W9-BBM-231

CREATIVE ACCESSORIES FOR THE HOME

76 Projects & Ideas

The Home Decorating Institute™

Copyright © 1993 Cy DeCosse Incorporated 5900 Green Oak Drive Minnetonka, Minnesota 55343
1-800-328-3895 All rights reserved Printed in U.S.A.

Library of Congress Cataloging-in-Publication Data Creative accessories for the home. p. cm. — (Arts & crafts for home decorating) Includes index. ISBN 0-86573-359-7 ISBN 0-86573-360-0 (pbk.)   1. House furnishings. 2. Interior decoration--Amateurs' manuals. I. Cy DeCosse Incorporated. II. Series.   TT157.C715 1993 745—dc20   93-18665 CIP

CONTENTS

Accessorizing Your Home

Baskets, Boxes & Trays

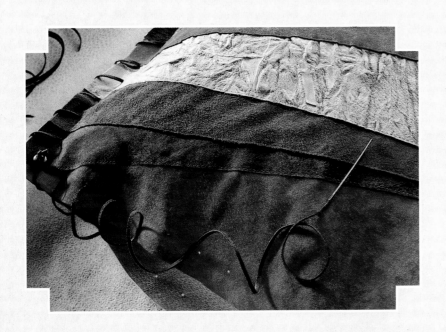

From Fabric & Leather

Clocks, Frames, Ceramics & More

ACCESSORIZING YOUR HOME

Accessories are the most personal part of decorating, often giving a room its unique character.

Accessories that have been handcrafted reflect your personality and allow you to customize items to blend with your decorating scheme. Create accessories with heirloom appeal by learning a new craft, such as rug hooking, basket weaving, or Hardanger embroidery. Or personalize accessories simply by embellishing purchased items, such as baskets, frames, and candles.

Baskets, boxes, and trays provide decorative accents as well as storage space. Make twig baskets, textural rag or leather baskets, and reed market baskets. Add whimsical painted designs or classic wood moldings to boxes. Embellish a tray with a tortoiseshell or gilded finish; or assemble a simple slatted tray, painting or staining it to match your decorating scheme.

Display customized clocks, frames, and ceramics on tables and shelves. Easy-to-assemble clock movements allow you to create a variety of clock styles. Frames can be embellished to complement your decorating scheme. Clear glass plates become unique decoupage art plates when backed with decorative papers, and plain ceramics become personalized accents when embellished with ceramic paints or mosaic tiles.

Use easy double-flange or haberdashery pillows to add interest to sofas and chairs. These versatile pillows can be used in any room in your home.

Any of these accessories can give a fresh look to an older home or add a personal touch to a new one.

All information in this book has been tested; however, because skill levels and conditions vary, the publisher disclaims any liability for unsatisfactory results. Follow the manufacturers' instructions for tools and materials used to complete these projects. The publisher is not responsible for any injury or damage caused by the improper use of tools, materials, or information in this publication.

Baskets,
Boxes & Trays

TWIG BASKETS

Perfect for a country setting or an eclectic style, these rustic twig baskets are assembled easily using a simple stacking method of construction. Since the baskets are made from gathered twigs, the only purchased materials are the wire nails.

Gather the twigs from a wooded area, looking for twigs that are straight and have a smooth bark. Willow is popular for twig baskets because its high moisture content makes it flexible and prevents it from splitting, but many other woods may also be used. Select twigs with a diameter of ⅜" to ¾" (1 to 2 cm), depending on the desired finished size of the basket. You may gather twigs that have fallen to the ground or cut branches from living trees.

If you plan to have a handle on the basket, you will need to cut that branch from a living tree, selecting one that can be bent into the curved shape without cracking. Plan to use the branch soon after it has been cut to prevent it from drying out.

When nailing two twigs together, select a nail that is no longer than the combined diameter of the two twigs. As you stack the twigs to form the sides, you may use a longer nail, because you will be nailing into the twig below as well as into the two being joined. To prevent the small-diameter nails from bending, support the nail with your thumb and forefinger; this is especially important if you are using hardwood twigs. It is also helpful to tap the nail lightly to avoid bending it.

MATERIALS

- Straight twigs with a smooth bark.
- Wire nails or brads in ⅝", ¾", and 1" (1.5, 2, and 2.5 cm) lengths.
- Hand saw; pruning shears; tack hammer.

Twisted handle *is made from intertwined, small-diameter branches of dogwood. Each branch of the handle is nailed into the basket twigs.*

Basket with dividers *organizes and displays kitchen items. The twig dividers were stacked, row by row, as the basket sides were assembled.*

HOW TO MAKE A TWIG BASKET

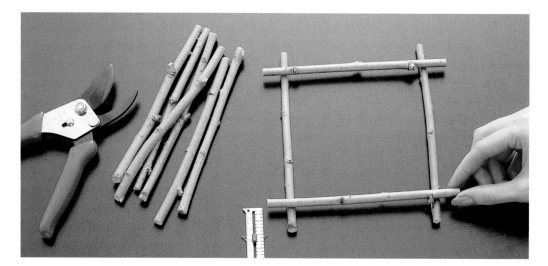

1 Cut twigs to the desired lengths. Lay two twigs on the work surface parallel to each other. Lay two more twigs on top of and perpendicular to the first two; overlap the twigs about 1" (2.5 cm) at corners.

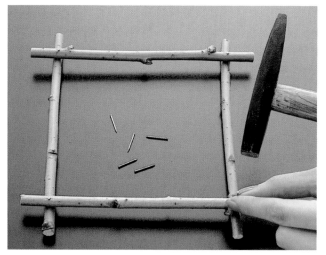

2 Nail the twigs together at intersecting corners, using nails of appropriate length.

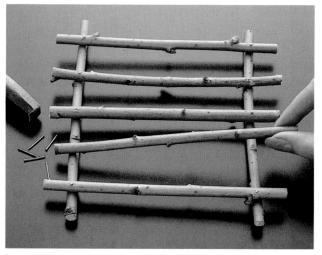

3 Lay twigs for the bottom of the basket perpendicular to first two twigs, spacing them about 1¼" to 1½" (3.2 to 3.8 cm) apart. Nail in place.

4 Lay two twigs perpendicular to the last row of twigs to begin building the sides of the basket. Nail in place at intersections, using 1" (2.5 cm) nails.

5 Add twigs, two at a time, laying them perpendicular to each previous row; nail in place, using 1" (2.5 cm) nails. Continue until the desired height is reached.

HOW TO ADD A HANDLE TO A TWIG BASKET

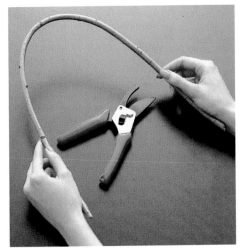

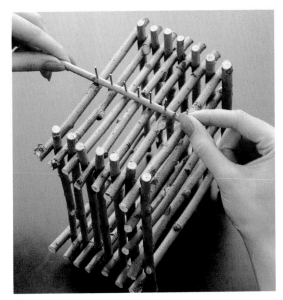

1 Cut branch to desired length for handle. Bend the branch to determine in which direction it bends more easily.

2 Place handle on center of one side of basket, with cut end of branch even with bottom of the basket. Press nails of appropriate length into handle where it intersects twigs of basket.

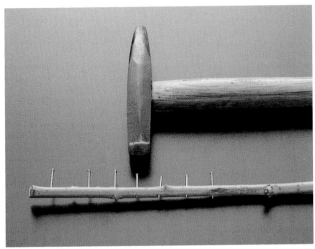

3 Lay handle on sturdy work surface; drive nails through the diameter of the handle.

4 Reposition the handle on the basket; nail in place.

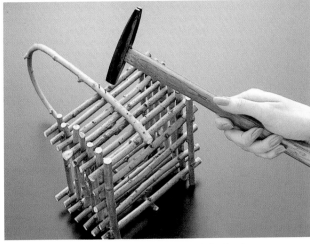

5 Bend the handle to the other side of the basket. Repeat steps 2 to 4.

6 Nail the handle again through each twig (arrow), from the inside of the basket, using side of hammer, if necessary.

MARKET BASKETS

The distinctive quality of a handmade basket adds a warm, decorative accent to any room. An easy-to-make market basket, sturdy enough to use for generations, can be completed in about three hours. The base, or bottom, of the basket measures about 6" × 10" (15 × 25.5 cm), and the sides are about 4½" (11.5 cm) high. The sturdy, wooden D-handle also doubles as a support for the market basket.

Basket materials are available from many fiber-art stores and craft stores as well as from mail-order suppliers. The reeds are made pliable by soaking them in warm water before weaving; a soaking time of three to five minutes is sufficient for most reeds. Determine the right and wrong sides of flat reeds as on page 14, step 2. When weaving baskets, place the right sides of the reeds to the outside of the basket.

The reeds may be left natural or stained in a wood tone or decorator color. Water-based basket stains or wood stains may be used; stains that contain a sealer add a protective finish to the basket. Solid-colored baskets are stained after the basket is completed. Multicolored baskets like those on pages 18 and 19 can be made by staining the reeds before weaving; test the stain to be sure it will not streak when the reeds are soaked. You may want to make a solid-colored basket, to become familiar with the techniques, before designing and weaving a multicolored basket.

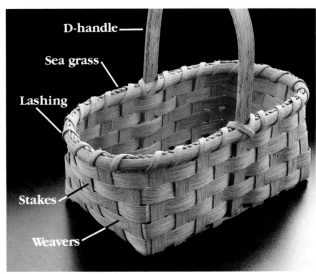

Market basket has a sturdy *D-handle*. Basket construction starts by weaving flat reeds to form the base, or bottom. These flat reeds are then upset, or turned up, to form the *stakes* for the sides of the basket; flat reeds, called *weavers*, are woven between the stakes, forming the sides. Two oval reeds are placed at the upper edge to form the rim; this provides an attractive edge and adds stability. *Sea grass* is inserted at the top of the rim, filling the space between the oval reeds, for a decorative finish. The rim is secured by wrapping it with a narrow oval reed; this reed, and the process of wrapping it, are referred to as *lashing*.

MATERIALS

- 6" × 10" (15 × 25.5 cm) D-handle.
- ⅝" (1.5 cm) flat reed, for stakes and weavers.
- ½" (1.3 cm) flat reed, for weaver.
- ½" (1.3 cm) flat oval reed, for rim.

- Sea grass, for rim filler.
- ¼" (6 mm) flat oval reed, for lashing.
- Reed cutter or utility scissors.
- Awl.

- Clothespins.
- Water-based basket stain or wood stain, optional; paintbrush or sponge applicator, for applying the stain.

HOW TO MAKE A MARKET BASKET

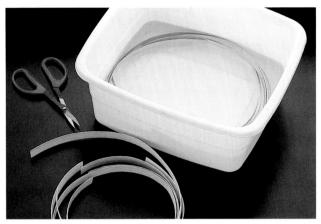

1 Cut ⅝" (1.5 cm) flat reed into five 25" (63.5 cm) lengths and eight 21" (53.5 cm) lengths; these will be used to form the base and stakes. Soak strips in warm water for about 3 minutes.

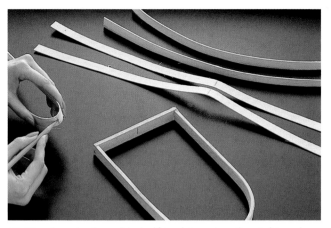

2 Bend soaked reed in half to determine the right and wrong sides; right side remains smooth, while wrong side splinters and appears hairy. Mark the centers of 25" (63.5 cm) reeds on wrong side, using pencil. Mark center of handle bottom on inside.

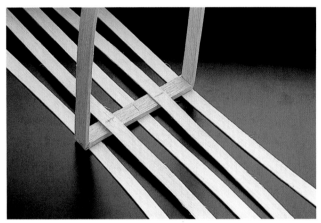

3 Position three marked strips under handle and two strips over handle, with right sides down and center marks at handle. Strips should be evenly spaced, with center strip aligned with center mark on handle and outside strips even with edge of handle.

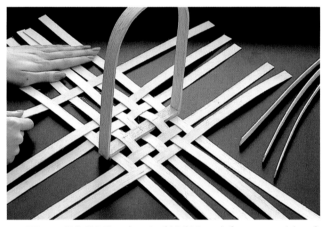

4 Weave 21" (53.5 cm) strip ½" (1.3 cm) from one side of handle, weaving under, over, under, over, and under the base reeds. Repeat with a second strip on opposite side of handle. Continue weaving, alternating sides, until four strips are woven on each side of handle.

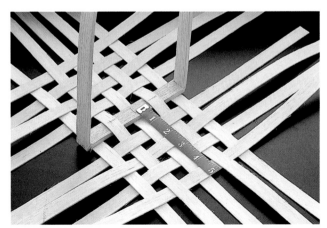

5 Adjust spacing of strips as necessary, so distance from center of handle to outside edge of last woven strip measures 5" (12.5 cm). Base size is 6" × 10" (15 × 25.5 cm).

6 Upset the sides by bending each stake toward the inside of the basket, rewetting reeds, if necessary.

7 Soak coil of ⅝" (1.5 cm) flat reed to be used as weavers. Center the end of reed over outside of first stake before handle; clamp with clothespin. Weave strip under handle and continue weaving to first corner.

8 Pinch reed gently at the corner to shape basket. Continue weaving to starting point; clamp as necessary.

9 Cut reed even with center of the second stake beyond handle.

10 Weave over the starting end of the weaver, then under handle; the cut end of the weaver will be concealed by the stake after it is upset.

11 Turn basket around to opposite side; weave second row, beginning in center of handle and weaving under first stake. At end, cut reed even with third stake beyond handle and weave over the starting end; then finish weaving the reed.

12 Continue weaving, alternating sides, to complete five rows of ⅝" (1.5 cm) flat reed; three rows will start before handle on one side, and two rows will start at handle on the opposite side. Allow top three rows to be rounded at corners. Using awl, compress the rows for a tight, even weave.

13 Cut strip of ½" (1.3 cm) flat reed to measurement around top of basket plus 4" (10 cm); soak. Weave a sixth row, starting at center of handle.

(Continued)

14 Cut the inner stakes even with the upper edge of the reed.

15 Bend outer stakes to the inside, rewetting them as necessary. Trim stakes at an angle; tuck them under the weaver, third row from the top, concealing pointed end.

16 Cut two strips of ½" (1.3 cm) flat oval reed to the measurement around the top of the basket plus 4" (10 cm); soak. Beginning about 1" (2.5 cm) before handle (arrow), wrap the reed around outside of the basket, with flat side of reed against top row of weaving; clamp with clothespins. Trim reed at an angle, at center of handle; the cut edge will be concealed with the lashing.

17 Position remaining strip of flat oval reed on inside of basket, against top row of weaving, overlapping ends at the opposite side of basket.

18 Cut one strip of sea grass and position it between the reeds at top of basket on one side. Repeat for other side.

19 Cut a strip of ¼" (6 mm) flat oval reed about 90" (229 cm) long, to be used for lashing; soak. Starting on side where inner rim overlaps, tuck end of lashing under lower edge of inner rim.

20 Insert lashing under rim, between the handle and stake, passing it from inside of basket to outside; if necessary, use awl to separate reeds so lashing can be inserted. Pull the lashing snug.

21 Wrap the lashing up and over rim and through next space between stakes; continue lashing around the basket to handle on opposite side.

22 Bring the lashing diagonally across the handle on outside of basket; from inside of basket, insert the lashing under rim directly below the place where the lashing crosses the top of the rim.

23 Bring the lashing diagonally across handle on the outside and inside; reinsert the lashing through the previous space to outside of basket.

24 Continue lashing to the opposite side of the basket; make an X over handle on outside of basket.

25 Cut lashing at an angle, and tuck the cut end under weaver below handle on inside of basket.

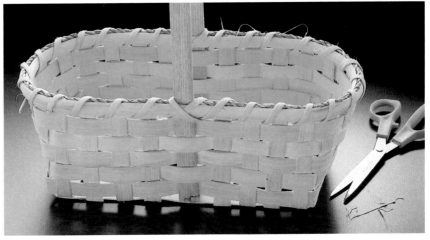

26 Allow basket to dry thoroughly. Trim loose hairs. Apply stain to basket, if desired; stain may be thinned with water, if necessary.

MORE IDEAS FOR MARKET BASKETS

Stained weavers *contrast with the stakes, creating a simple, yet colorful, design.*

Weavers in graduated widths *are used for this stained basket. Starting at the base of stakes, weave five rows of ¼" (6 mm) flat reed, three rows of ½" (1.3 cm) reed, and one row of ⅝" (1.5 cm) reed before adding the rim.*

Sea grass, *woven between ½" (1.3 cm) weavers, adds texture. Soak the sea grass before weaving. Because the sea grass is too heavy to overlap, begin and end the weaving inside the basket, allowing the ends to extend.*

Center band is composed of a ⅝" (1.5 cm) reed in dark blue, bordered by ¼" (6 mm) natural reeds. Natural sea grass edges the top of the basket, and the remaining reeds, stained light blue, are ½" (1.3 cm) wide.

Larger basket is made using an 8" × 12" (20.5 × 30.5 cm) D-handle and has a woven base of 8" × 12" (20.5 × 30.5 cm). From ⅝" (1.5 cm) flat reed, cut seven 32" (81.5 cm) lengths and ten 28" (71 cm) lengths for the base and stakes. For the weavers, cut seven 46" (117 cm) lengths.

Contrasting rim and weavers accent this market basket. Starting at the base of the stakes, weave two rows of ⅝" (1.5 cm) flat reed, three rows of ¼" (6 mm) reed, and two rows of ⅝" (1.5 cm) reed before adding the rim.

DECORATING
BASKETS

Add your personal touch to purchased baskets by topping them lavishly with ivy or garland, then adding embellishments, such as latex fruit or silk flowers.

For a more rustic look, encircle a basket with bundles of wheat, and tie it with raffia. Or trim the rim of the basket with moss, fallen birch bark, and other dried naturals. For a romantic touch, simply weave a fancy ribbon into an open-weave basket.

Baskets with lids can be made into decorative accessories that provide hidden storage space. Top the lid with silk flowers or preserved leaves. Or embellish the lid with items that reflect a hobby, such as beach-combed seashells, sewing notions, or fishing tackle.

Most items can be secured to baskets using a hot glue gun and glue sticks. For temporary placement, you can secure items with wire or floral adhesive clay.

Moss trims the rim of a basket, with a fanciful bird's nest used as an accent.

Ivy tops this birch basket and twists around the handle. The clusters of latex berries complete the arrangement.

Woven ribbon adds a simple but elegant touch to an open-weave metal basket.

Dried naturals, including pods and preserved leaves, add interest to the lid of the basket at right.

Wheat stems, bundled together, encircle a basket (opposite). Raffia adds a touch of country.

HOW TO MAKE AN IVY-TOPPED BASKET

MATERIALS

- Basket.
- Silk ivy vines or artificial garland.
- Embellishments, such as latex fruit or silk flowers.
- Wire and wire cutter; or hot glue gun and glue sticks.

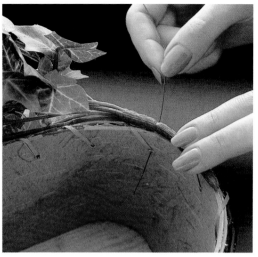

1 Cut several vines of ivy or a length of artificial garland, and arrange around top of basket; secure with wire or hot glue.

2 Twist ivy around handle of basket, if desired; secure with wire or hot glue. Arrange and secure latex fruit or silk flowers.

HOW TO MAKE A WHEAT-STEM BASKET

MATERIALS

- Wheat with long stems.
- Rubber bands.
- Raffia.
- Old scissors.
- Hot glue gun and glue sticks.

1 Cut several wheat stems to desired lengths, using old scissors. Group stems in bundles; secure with rubber bands.

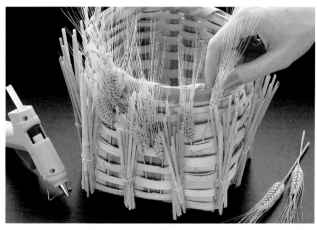

2 Secure bundles to sides of basket, using hot glue. Add heads of wheat, tucking stem ends into or between the bundles.

3 Tie a length of raffia around the basket, concealing rubber bands.

HOW TO MAKE A MOSS-RIMMED BASKET

MATERIALS

- Moss.
- Embellishments, such as lichens, fallen birch bark, twigs, and other dried naturals; small craft bird's nest, optional.
- Hot glue gun and glue sticks.

1 Secure pieces of moss to basket rim, using hot glue, applying it to both the inside and the outside of rim.

2 Glue lichens and other dried naturals to moss, scattering them around the rim. Glue bird's nest in place, if desired.

HOW TO EMBELLISH A BASKET WITH WOVEN RIBBON

MATERIALS

- Open-weave basket.
- Ribbon and bow.
- Large-eyed needle.
- Wire, for securing bow.

1 Thread ribbon into a large-eyed needle. Weave ribbon in and out of the basket.

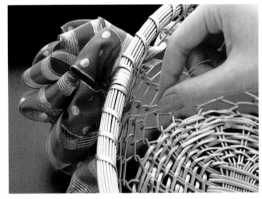

2 Wire bow to one side of basket, concealing ends of woven ribbon.

HOW TO EMBELLISH A BASKET WITH A LID

MATERIALS

- Basket with lid.
- Embellishments, such as dried seed pods, stones, and preserved leaves.
- Hot glue gun and glue sticks.

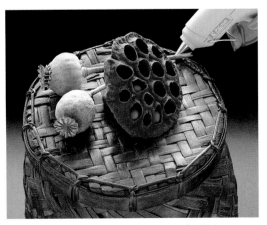

1 Arrange dominant or larger embellishments on lid of basket as desired. Secure with hot glue. Some items can be used as a base for smaller items to add height to the arrangement.

2 Add secondary or smaller embellishments, stacking items as desired.

RAG BASKETS

Rag baskets are simple to construct and can be made in many sizes, from tabletop baskets to large floor baskets. Large baskets with lids can be used to store items such as toys, linens, and seasonal clothing. The baskets are made by wrapping narrow strips of fabric around basket cording as it is coiled into shape. Wooden handles may be added at the sides, or handles may be shaped from the cording.

The basket cording is available in ½" or ¾" (1.3 or 2 cm) diameter at craft and quilting shops as well as through mail-order suppliers. Use the narrow cording for small baskets and the wider cording for large floor baskets.

Traditionally made from leftover fabrics, rag baskets can also be made from discarded clothing, bed sheets, or newly purchased fabrics. Depending on the look you want to achieve, use the same fabric throughout the entire basket or combine several fabrics.

The fabric and cording yardages vary greatly with the size of the baskets. Shown opposite, the basket with the lid is 15" (38 cm) high and 17" (43 cm) in diameter; it requires 11 yd. (10.12 m) fabric and 50 yd. (46 m) of ¾" (2 cm) basket cording. The smaller basket is 10" (25.5 cm) high and 8" (20.5 cm) in diameter; it requires 3½ yd. (3.2 m) fabric and 20 yd. (18.4 m) of ½" (1.3 cm) cording. Approximate yardages are also given for the baskets on pages 28 and 29. To determine the amount of each fabric needed, divide the total yardage by the number of fabrics to be used.

MATERIALS

- Firmly woven, mediumweight fabrics, such as cotton broadcloth.
- Basket cording in ½" (1.3 cm) diameter for small baskets or ¾" (2 cm) diameter for large baskets.
- Tapestry needle, size 13.
- Masking tape or duct tape.
- Rotary cutter and cutting mat.
- Wooden rings, for handles, optional.
- Large wooden bead, for top of lid, optional.

HOW TO MAKE A RAG BASKET

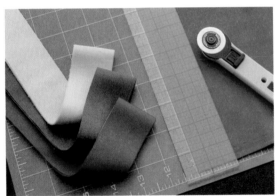

1 Cut fabric on crosswise grain into 1½" (3.8 cm) strips, about 45" (115 cm) long.

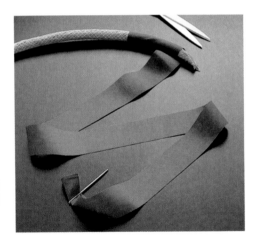

2 Taper end of cording with scissors. Thread fabric strip into a tapestry needle. Beginning about 5" (12.5 cm) from end of cording, wrap unthreaded end of strip tightly around cording, wrapping away from you, almost to end.

3 Fold end of the cording to make a loop; wrap fabric twice over both cords to secure the loop, leaving small hole. Continue wrapping strip away from you around 3" (7.5 cm) of the uncovered cording, with the uncovered cording to the right.

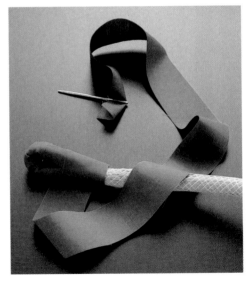

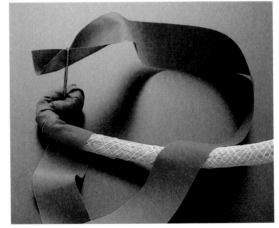

4 Begin coiling the cording into a circle. Secure coil by inserting needle into center hole and pulling fabric through firmly; repeat.

(Continued)

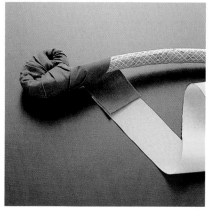

5 Wrap strip around the uncovered cording about three times, wrapping away from you, with the uncovered cording to the right. Secure coil by inserting needle into center hole and pulling fabric firmly; secure coil a second time.

6 Wrap strip around the uncovered cording about three times; splice strips as necessary by lapping new strip over end of previous strip.

7 Secure coil with a joining wrap by inserting needle between rows of previously wrapped cording and pulling the fabric firmly; repeat. If desired, stabilize the joining wrap as in steps 8 and 9; or omit these steps and proceed to step 10.

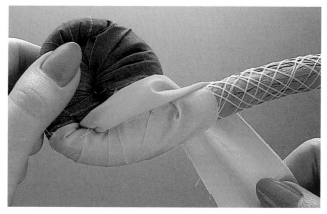

8 Insert strip between wrapped and unwrapped cords; then bring it up just before the joining wrap (arrow); this will form a loop on the opposite side of the basket.

9 Bring strip down between wrapped and unwrapped cords. Continue by wrapping away from you.

10 Splice cording, when necessary, by tapering ends of cords for about 4" (10 cm). Overlap ends, and wrap with masking tape.

11 Wrap and secure the coil until the bottom is desired diameter. Start to build up the sides by laying cording on top of outer row.

12 Construct sides of basket by building up rows of cording. If desired, taper sides by gradually spiraling larger coils. If desired, add handles and knob (opposite).

13 Cut cording at an angle when the basket is desired height; wrap with fabric strip. Secure end of cording to the previous coil by wrapping several times with fabric strip. Conceal end of fabric strip, trimming excess.

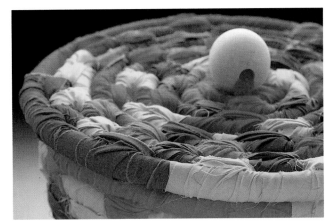

14 Make a lid, if desired, using the same method as for bottom of basket, with diameter of lid slightly larger than basket top. Add wooden knob (below).

HOW TO ADD WOODEN HANDLES & KNOB

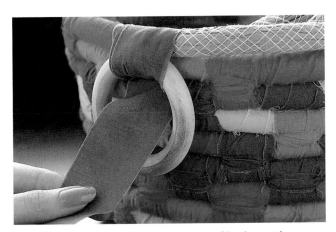

Handles. Secure wooden ring to side of basket with a joining wrap, as in step 7; wrap fabric around ring four times for added strength. Continue halfway around basket; attach second handle.

Knob. Thread a fabric strip through a large wooden bead; position at center of lid. Insert ends of fabric strip through lid to underside; knot to secure.

HOW TO ADD FABRIC HANDLES

Handles at top.
Secure coil with a joining wrap, as in step 7. Wrap cording for 5" to 6" (12.5 to 15 cm), and shape it to form a handle. Secure with joining wrap. Continue halfway around basket, and make second handle.

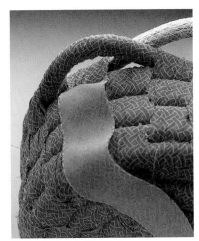

Handles at sides.
Follow step at left, as for handles at top of basket; then wrap next row until you reach first handle. Secure basket under the handle with a joining wrap that wraps around one or two coils, as shown. Continue the row to the second handle; secure.

MORE IDEAS
FOR RAG BASKETS

Decorative cords and beads embellish this small basket. This basket measures 5" (12.5 cm) high and is 9" (23 cm) in diameter; it requires about 1 yd. (0.95 m) fabric and 8 yd. (7.35 m) of ½" (1.3 cm) basket cording.

Floor baskets add textural interest to a room. The larger basket is 19" (48.5 cm) high and 11" (28 cm) in diameter; it requires 4½ yd. (4.15 m) fabric and 25 yd. (23 m) of ¾" (2 cm) cording. The smaller basket is 9" (23 cm) high and 13" (33 cm) in diameter at the widest point; it requires 3 yd. (2.75 m) fabric and 16 yd. (14.72 m) of ¾" (2 cm) cording.

Fabric strips are tied randomly around the joining wraps after the entire basket is coiled. This basket is 5" (12.5 cm) high and 9" (23 cm) in diameter at the base; it requires 1⅝ yd. (1.5 m) fabric and 12 yd. (11.04 m) of ½" (1.3 cm) cording.

Matching fabric is used to coordinate a flat basket with the quilt in this bedroom. This basket is 3" (7.5 cm) high and 12" (30.5 cm) in diameter at the top; it requires 1¾ yd. (1.6 m) fabric and 8 yd. (7.35 m) of ½" (1.3 cm) cording.

Hamper with lid (right) is 21" (53.5 cm) high and 17" (43 cm) in diameter at the base; it requires 15 yd. (13.8 m) fabric and 64 yd. (58.88 m) of ¾" (2 cm) cording.

Dress up simple, unfinished wooden boxes with decorative moldings and medallions. Available in a variety of styles, these trims may be glued to the sides of the box and on the lid.

Craft stores that stock miniature supplies have a variety of moldings and medallions for doll houses. These decorative trims are made of soft wood and are easy to work with. Specialty woodworking stores carry cabinetry trims in narrow widths that are also suitable for trimming boxes.

Moldings are easily cut using a miter box and backsaw, or even the small miter box and backsaw intended for use with miniature moldings. Select a backsaw that has a fine-tooth blade.

Many trims may be secured simply by gluing the trims in place and clamping them until dry; place a scrap of lumber or a felt pad under the clamps to protect the wood. For a secure bond and to reduce the need for clamping, you may want to insert brads at the corners of the moldings.

Trims may be stained or painted to match or contrast with the box. If contrasting trims are desired, paint or stain the trims before attaching them to the box.

MATERIALS

- Unfinished wooden box.
- Decorative moldings and medallions.
- Wood glue; emery board or sandpaper.
- Miter box and backsaw.
- Clamps, optional.
- Brads and nail set, optional.
- Stain or paint as desired; wood putty to match stain.

Narrow moldings and small medallions *are available at stores specializing in miniatures and at woodworking stores.*

Wooden boxes, *trimmed with moldings and medallions, can be stained, as shown above, or painted in contrasting colors, as shown opposite.*

HOW TO ADD WOOD TRIMS TO A BOX

1 Miter moldings for sides of box at front corners; leave excess length on the molding strips. Miter one corner on molding for the front of the box, leaving excess length.

2 Position mitered front and side molding strips at one corner. Mark the finished length of the front piece; mark the angle of the cut. Cut miter. Repeat for side piece.

3 Reposition moldings; mark second side piece, and miter to fit.

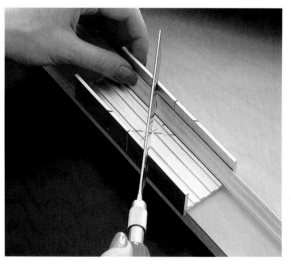

4 Miter one corner on molding for the back of box, leaving excess length. Position with side strip; mark length of opposite corner. Cut miter.

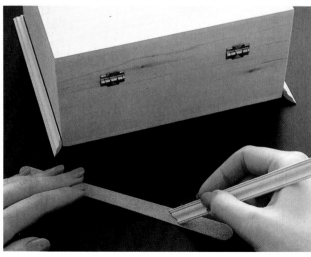

5 Reposition moldings; sand corners, using emery board or sandpaper, as necessary for proper fit.

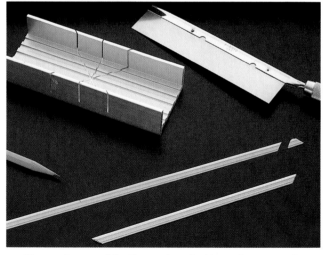

6 Determine outside dimensions for inset frame. Mark one length on the outer edge of molding; cut inside miters at each end. Cut a second strip for opposite side of frame, making sure lengths are even.

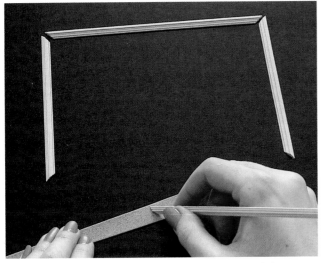

7 Repeat to cut strips that fit remaining sides of the inset frame. Sand corners, using emery board or sandpaper, as necessary for proper fit.

8 Paint or stain box and wood trims, if contrasting trim is desired.

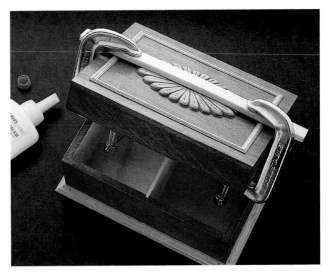

9 Predrill nail holes in hardwood moldings that will be secured with brads, using 1/16" (1.5 mm) drill bit. Apply bead of glue to back of moldings. Position on box; clamp until dry, or secure with brads.

10 Secure decorative wood medallions, if desired, using wood glue; clamp until dry. To protect wood trims from clamps, use a scrap of lumber as shown.

11 Countersink brads, using nail set. Paint or stain the box as desired; if stain is used, fill the nail holes with matching putty.

TROMPE L'OEIL BOXES

Decoratively painted wooden boxes can accent desks, countertops, and end tables as well as provide needed storage for small items. Designs painted in trompe l'œil, which means "fool the eye," add whimsy to simple wooden boxes. On the following pages, the instructions and any necessary patterns are given for three designs with a trompe l'œil effect. Choose either a box tied with a ribbon bow, a wrapped parcel, or a stationery box.

Use unfinished wooden boxes with hinges, available at craft stores in a variety of sizes. Or decorate boxes found at garage sales or gift shops. If you choose an unfinished box, sand it as necessary, and use a primer before applying the base coat of paint. If painting a box with a varnished surface, lightly sand the surfaces to ensure good paint adhesion.

Use good-quality brushes to achieve even edges and fine lines. Test the paints for proper consistency; a detailed design is often easier to achieve with slightly thinned paints.

To protect the painted finish on the box, apply an aerosol acrylic sealer, available in matte and gloss finishes. A matte finish is recommended for the parcel box; either a matte or a gloss finish is appropriate for the bow and stationery boxes.

MATERIALS

- Wooden box.
- Graphite paper.
- Acrylic paints.
- Artist brushes, such as a flat shader and a liner.
- Fine permanent-ink pen.
- Stationery, to use as pattern guide for stationery box.
- Aerosol acrylic sealer.

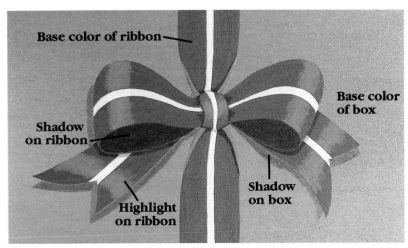

Trompe l'œil designs (below) are painted on wooden boxes to create a stationery box, a wrapped parcel, and a box tied with a ribbon bow.

Highlights and shadows add a dimensional effect to painted designs. To paint the highlights, mix white paint with the design's base color. For example, add highlights to a red bow by mixing white paint with red. To paint the shadows, use a darker shade of the base color or mix black with the base color. For example, use a darker red for the shadows inside the loop of the bow; use a darker brown for the shadows that are on top of the box.

HOW TO PAINT A BOW BOX

1 Apply base coats of paint; allow to dry. Transfer bow design (page 39) to top of box, using graphite paper.

2 Tape box closed at ends. Using pencil, lightly mark ribbon placement by extending lines from bow, 1⅛" (2.8 cm) wide, along top, front, and back of box. For stripes of ribbon, mark lines ½" (1.3 cm) from ribbon placement lines.

3 Paint outer stripes of ribbon using artist's brush, such as a flat shader. Allow paint to dry.

4 Paint the center stripe of the ribbon; allow to dry.

5 Mix a lighter shade of the colors used for the ribbon, using white paint. Highlight the ribbon as shown, to add dimension.

6 Paint a shadow effect on the ribbon as shown, using a darker shade of the ribbon color and thinning the paint for a translucent effect. Paint shadow effect on box as shown, using a darker shade of box color and thinning the paint. Apply aerosol acrylic sealer, if desired.

HOW TO PAINT A PARCEL BOX

1 Apply base coats of paint; allow to dry. Tape box closed. Using pencil, lightly mark fold lines of paper as shown, on opposite sides of box.

2 Mark placement for string along sides and top of box, drawing knot at center of box top.

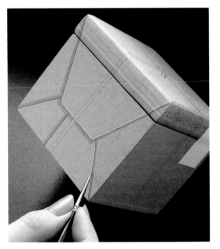

3 Paint fold lines of paper, using darker shade of box color; do not paint where string will overlap fold lines. Allow to dry. Paint highlights and shadows as shown.

4 Apply white paint along marked lines for string; allow to dry. Paint highlights and shadows on one side of string; paint the center knot detail.

5 Mark area for the postage stamp; transfer stamp design (page 39), using graphite paper.

6 Paint stamp, using thinned paint. When dry, paint the lettering and price on stamp, using a permanent-ink pen.

7 Transfer and paint additional labels (page 39) on box, taking care not to paint over the string. Apply aerosol acrylic sealer, if desired.

HOW TO PAINT A STATIONERY BOX

1 Paint or stain box; allow to dry. Mark lines for belt, 1" the (2.5 cm) apart and centered on box, around the top, front, and back. Paint belt, using brown paint; allow paint to dry. Transfer belt details, key, and eyeglasses (opposite) onto box, using graphite paper. Mark placement of eyeglass chain. Mark ¼" (6 mm) strips around the box at lower edge of the top and 1" (2.5 cm) from lower edge of box.

2 Paint the strips around the box, using black paint. Paint the buckle, key, and eyeglasses, using gold paint; for eyeglass chain, use wooden end of brush to paint dots. Paint highlights and shadows of items as shown.

3 Complete belt details, and paint ribbon for key. Paint highlights and shadows as shown.

4 Tape stationery to the top of the box; trace to mark placement. Mark ¼" (6 mm) border on top of box, 1" (2.5 cm) from edges.

5 Paint and outline the stationery. Paint postage stamp as on page 37, steps 5 and 6. Write address on envelope, using permanent-ink marking pen.

6 Transfer fountain pen and stationery design (opposite). Paint border on top of box, fountain pen, and stationery design, using black and gold paints. Paint shadows and highlights. Apply aerosol acrylic sealer, if desired.

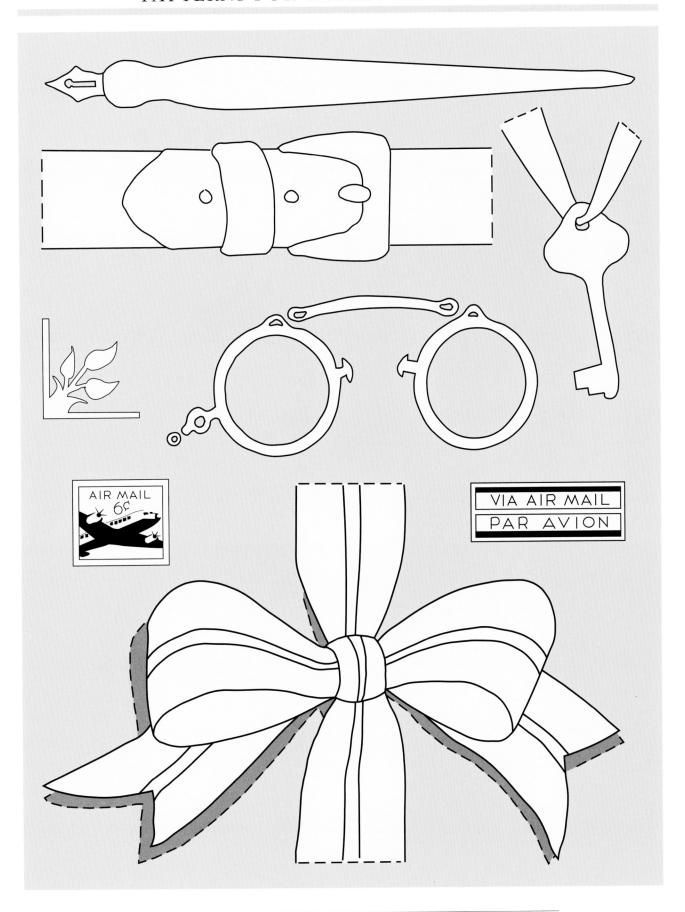

AIR MAIL
6¢

VIA AIR MAIL
PAR AVION

DECORATIVE
TRAYS

Turn plain trays into stunning accessories by applying a decorative finish. Choose from simplified gilding or a tortoiseshell finish.

Oil-based paints, such as Japan paints, are used for both techniques. Japan paints, available in small containers, are sold at art supply stores and with stenciling supplies at many paint stores.

Gilded designs are applied using precut Mylar® stencils and metallic powder. Apply the metallic powder over a surface of tacky varnish. The result is a stenciled surface that is much smoother and more subtle than that achieved by stenciling with metallic paints. Metallic powders are available at art supply stores in a wide range of colors, from silvery white to rich bronze gold.

A tortoiseshell finish is achieved by streaking thinned varnish stains over a painted base. An orange-red paint, often called barn red, is used for the base coat, and varnish stains in dark oak and black are used for the streaking. The dark oak varnish stain is available at paint and hardware stores, and the black is created by adding black artist's oil color.

Select a tray with smooth, flat surfaces, lightly sanding any prevarnished surfaces to ensure paint adhesion. It is easiest to apply a tortoiseshell finish to a flat, horizontal surface. For this reason, paint the sides of the tray in a solid color and apply the tortoiseshell finish to the bottom only; tape off the sides before working on the bottom of the tray.

Purchased trays *can have a painted tortoiseshell finish, as shown above. Or they can be decorated with a stenciled gilded design and then varnished, as shown opposite.*

HOW TO GILD A TRAY

MATERIALS

- Oil-based paint, such as Japan paint, for base coat.
- Oil-based clear varnish, in gloss or semigloss finish.
- Metallic powder in desired color.
- Precut Mylar® stencil.
- Masking tape.
- Scrap of velvet or chamois leather.

1 Apply a base coat of oil-based paint to a clean, prepared surface; allow to dry. Apply a coat of varnish. Allow varnish to dry about 3 to 5 hours, until slightly tacky; at this time, if the corner of stencil is pressed against the varnish, stencil can be removed with a slight pull, but will leave no mark.

2 Pour a small amount of metallic powder into a bowl. Position stencil in desired location; cover surrounding area on tray by taping paper to stencil.

3 Wrap a scrap of velvet or chamois leather around index finger, wrapping it smoothly so there are no wrinkles or creases at fingertip. Dip wrapped finger into metallic powder; rub on a piece of paper to remove excess powder.

4 Gently rub area to be gilded, starting at the center and working out. As necessary, pick up more powder and reposition stencil. Remove stencil, and allow varnish to dry at least 24 hours.

5 Remove any powder outside design area by rubbing gently with mild abrasive cleanser. Wash the surface gently, using soapy water. Rinse and dry.

6 Seal the gilding by applying a coat of varnish; allow varnish to dry.

HOW TO APPLY A TORTOISESHELL FINISH TO A TRAY

MATERIALS

- Oil-based paints, such as Japan paints, in orange-red and black.
- Dark oak varnish stain, in gloss finish.
- Black artist's oil color in small tube.
- Mineral spirits.
- Two flat 2" (5 cm) paintbrushes; round artist's brush.
- Oil-based clear varnish, in gloss or semigloss finish, optional.
- Masking tape.

1 Apply black paint to sides of tray; allow to dry. Tape off inside lower edge of tray sides, using masking tape.

2 Apply base coat of orange-red paint to bottom of tray; allow to dry. Squeeze a small amount of black oil color into a bowl; dilute with dark oak varnish stain until mixture will flow, and set aside to be used in step 5.

3 Dilute dark oak varnish stain, about one part mineral spirits to two parts varnish; apply over base coat of paint, using flat paintbrush.

(Continued)

4 Brush irregular, diagonal zigzag strokes across the surface of the wet varnish.

5 Apply diluted black oil color from step 2 in irregular streaks, parallel to diagonal brush strokes and about 2" (5 cm) apart; use a pointed artist's brush and a sideways rolling motion. Allow the surface to harden for 1 to 2 minutes.

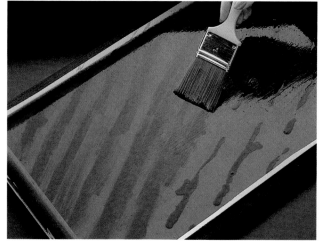

6 Stroke the bristle tips of a clean, dry paintbrush gently over the black streaks, in the same direction as they were painted; this will give wispy edges.

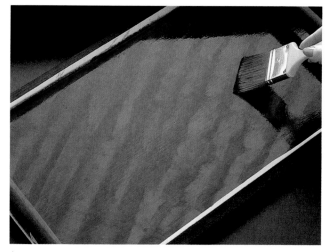

7 Repeat step 6, stroking in opposite diagonal direction; this merges some of the streaks. Repeat as necessary to even up the design, taking care not to darken all of the base color.

8 Allow surface to dry. For a more durable finish, apply a coat of clear varnish to bottom and sides of the tray.

MORE IDEAS FOR DECORATIVE TRAYS

Blonde tortoiseshell finish *is achieved by applying a base coat of metallic gold paint, followed by a dark oak varnish. Artist's oil colors in burnt umber and black are used for the streaked effect.*

Gilded tray *with two colors of metallic powder is achieved by using a stencil kit that contains a separate stencil plate for each metallic color.*

SLATTED
TRAYS

Black lacquered tray *is a sophisticated accent on a contemporary table. The stained and painted tray, opposite, has a country look.*

Simple in style, this tray is attractive as a decorative accessory on a buffet or side table and sturdy enough to use as a serving tray. The tray is built using stock screen molding and parting stop; simply cut the strips to length. The instructions that follow are for a tray that measures about 11¾" × 18" (30 × 46 cm); the dimensions can be easily changed for a custom size.

Screen molding, generally available in pine and oak, is used for the slats of the base and the runners on the bottom. Parting stop, generally available in pine only, is used for the sides and handles.

The tray may be either stained or painted. Or for another look, stain and paint may be used in combination. For example, if oak screen molding and pine parting stop are used in the same tray, you may prefer to stain the oak and paint the pine.

For ease in finishing, apply the paint or stain before assembling the tray. If you are painting the tray, apply a wood primer before applying a good-quality enamel paint. For a more durable finish on either a stained or painted tray, apply a final coat of nonyellowing varnish or polyurethane sealer.

MATERIALS

- 22 ft. (671 cm) of ¼" × ¾" (6 mm × 2 cm) pine or oak screen molding.
- 5 ft. (152.5 cm) of ½" × ¾" (1.3 × 2 cm) pine parting stop.
- Twelve 6 × 1" (2.5 cm) brass wood screws, for securing runners and handles.
- ¾" (2 cm) brads, for securing the slats.
- 180-grit or 220-grit sandpaper.

- Drill; ¹⁄₁₆" and ³⁄₃₂" drill bits; ⁹⁄₆₄" countersink bit.
- Coping saw; or miter box and backsaw.
- Phillips screwdriver.
- Wood glue.
- Wood stain, or wood primer and enamel paint.
- Nonyellowing varnish or polyurethane sealer, optional.

HOW TO MAKE A SLATTED TRAY

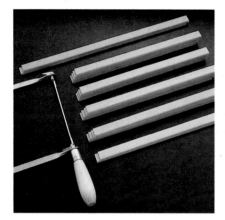

1 Cut 16 slats from screen molding in 11¾" (30 cm) lengths; you may want to cut two or three extra slats in case some split during assembly. Cut two bottom runners from the screen molding in 15¾" (40 cm) lengths.

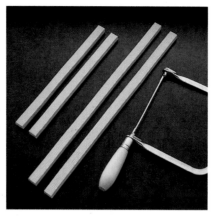

2 Cut two tray handles from parting stop in 11¾" (30 cm) lengths. Cut two tray sides from parting stop in 18" (46 cm) lengths. Round edges at cut ends of all strips by sanding them. Sand sides of strips as necessary. Apply stain, or apply primer and paint.

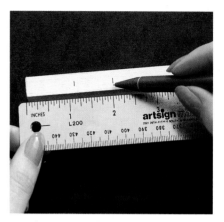

3 Place one side piece with the narrow side up. Using a pencil, lightly mark lines 1⅛" (2.8 cm) and 2" (5 cm) from ends; if markings are in center of strip, they will be less noticeable in finished tray. Repeat for remaining side piece.

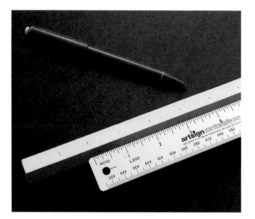

4 Mark the space between the two inner lines at 1" (2.5 cm) intervals. Repeat for remaining side piece.

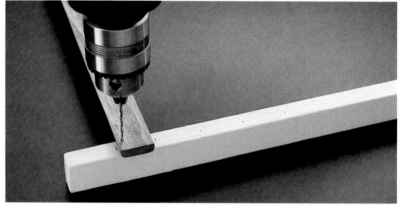

5 Position one tray slat, rounded side down, on side piece, with outer edge of slat aligned with end marking and end of slat extending ⅛" (3 mm) beyond edge of side. Predrill ¹⁄₁₆" (1.5 mm) hole for brad, offsetting hole to allow for later application of screw. Glue slat to side; secure with nail. Repeat for slat at opposite end of side piece.

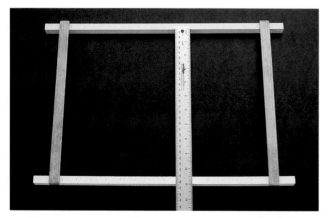

6 Secure remaining side piece to opposite ends of slats, as in step 5, making sure sides are parallel; distance between inside edges of sides is 10½" (27.8 cm).

7 Lay out 14 slats, ¼" (6 mm) apart, between end slats, using marked lines as guides; sides of slats should be ⅛" (3 mm) from marked lines.

8 Predrill and secure slats, securing one slat at a time; start at ends of tray, alternating from side to side, and work toward center. Brads need to be offset on sixth and eleventh slats.

9 Position bottom runners over slats, rounded side up, ⅛" (3 mm) from ends of slats. Predrill holes for screws into end slats, using 3⁄32" drill bit; drill countersink holes.

10 Predrill holes for screws into sixth and eleventh slats, as in step 9. Glue the runners to the slats; secure the screws, taking care not to overtighten them.

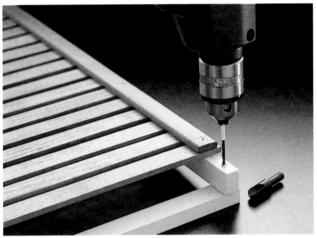

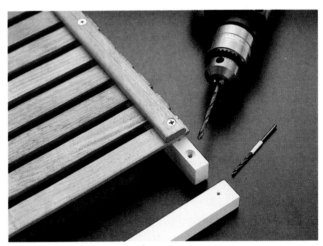

11 Position handles, centered under sides of tray as shown, about ⅛" (3 mm) from ends of side pieces. Predrill holes, 1" (2.5 cm) through the side pieces and handles, using 3⁄32" drill bit. Drill countersink holes, drilling no farther than necessary to sink screw heads.

12 Remove handles. Using 9⁄64" drill bit, drill clearance hole through sides only.

13 Reposition the handles, and secure with wood glue. Insert screws.

14 Apply nonyellowing varnish or polyurethane sealer, if desired.

From Fabric & Leather

DOUBLE-FLANGE
PILLOWS

Double-flange pillows have an understated look and exceptional versatility. Made from brocades and tapestries, they are elegant in a traditional setting, yet their streamlined design makes them equally elegant in contemporary prints and solids. Select floral prints of polished cotton, and these pillows are right at home in a country room. For these pillows, two mitered panels are stitched together along the inner edge of the border, creating a double flange. At the center of the pillow, a matching or contrasting fabric is tucked under the flange before the pillow front and pillow back are joined.

HOW TO SEW A DOUBLE-FLANGE PILLOW WITH AN INSERT

MATERIALS

- Fabric for pillow front and pillow back, including flange, yardage depending on size of project; for 14" (35.5 cm) pillow form and 2½" (6.5 cm) flange, you will need ¾ yd. (0.7 m) of 54" (137 cm) fabric.

- Fabric for insert at center of pillow; yardage depending on size of project; for 14" (35.5 cm) pillow form, you will need ⅝ yd. (0.6 m).

- Pillow form in desired size.

- Polyester fiberfill, for filling out corners.

CUTTING DIRECTIONS

The size of the inner portion of the pillow is equal to the size of the pillow form. To this measurement, add four times the desired width of the flange plus ½" (1.3 cm) for turning under the raw edges; cut two pieces of fabric this size, for the pillow front and pillow back. For example, for a 14" (35.5 cm) square pillow with a 2½" (6.5 cm) flange, use a 14" (35.5 cm) pillow form, and cut two pieces, each 24½" (62.3 cm) square. For the center insert, add twice the desired depth of the flange to the size of the pillow form; cut one piece of insert fabric.

1 Stitch scant ¼" (6 mm) from edges of pillow front. Fold edges to the wrong side; press just beyond the stitching line. On each side, press under desired depth of flange.

2 Open out the corner; fold diagonally so pressed folds match (arrows). Press diagonal fold.

3 Open out the corner. Fold through center of corner, right sides together. Stitch on diagonal foldline from step 2. Trim fabric at corner ¼" (6 mm) from stitching. Press seam open.

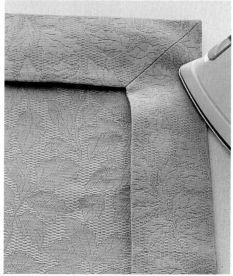

4 Press the flange in place, turning the corners right side out.

5 Place insert fabric on pillow front, tucking raw edges under flange; smooth, and pin in place.

6 Press under sides of pillow back, an amount equal to depth of flange plus ¼" (6 mm), so fabric on folded flange is right side up. Miter corners as in steps 2 to 4.

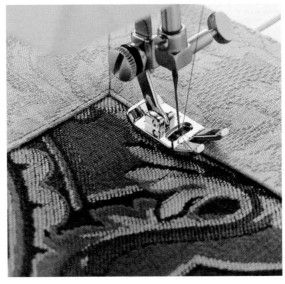

7 Place pillow front on pillow back, with mitered sides up, matching edges; pin.

8 Stitch around inner edge of flange, securing the insert; pivot at corners, and leave opening on one side for inserting pillow form.

9 Insert the pillow form; push fiberfill into the corners of the pillow as necessary to fill out pillow. Pin the opening closed; complete stitching on inner edge of flange.

MORE IDEAS FOR DOUBLE-FLANGE PILLOWS

Braid trim (page 58), like the wide, elegant braid on this pillow, adds definition to the inner edge of the flange. The trim is mitered at the corners for a professional finish.

The simple design of a double-flange pillow lends itself to a number of variations. For additional impact, embellish the pillows with decorative trims. Weave ribbon trims together for an elegant checked effect, or apply them diagonally across the pillow front, creating a free-form pattern. For a different look, trim the inner edge of the flanges with a decorative braid trim.

The center portion of the pillow can have a pieced fabric insert for added interest. Select several coordinating fabrics, piecing them together in either a planned or random design.

Pieced insert (page 59) can be sewn in either a planned design or in a random, patchwork design.

Woven insert made from iridescent ribbons adds impact to a double-flange pillow.

Diagonal trims (page 58) are positioned randomly for a creative effect. The printed fabrics used for these pillows reverse to solid black on the wrong side, making the contrasting flanges.

HOW TO SEW A DOUBLE-FLANGE PILLOW WITH A WOVEN INSERT

MATERIALS

- Fabric for pillow front and pillow back, including flange, yardage depending on size of project; for 14" (35.5 cm) pillow form and 2½" (6.5 cm) flange, you will need ¾ yd. (0.7 m) of 54" (137 cm) fabric.
- Trims, such as ribbons or braids.
- Pillow form in desired size.
- Polyester fiberfill, for filling out corners.

CUTTING DIRECTIONS

Cut pillow front and pillow back as on page 54.

Cut trims 1" (2.5 cm) longer than measurement of pillow form; this allows sufficient length for ¼" (6 mm) seam allowances and for weaving the trims.

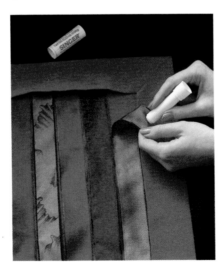

1 Follow steps 1 to 4 on page 54. Plan the placement of trims. Apply glue stick to ¼" (6 mm) seam allowance at one end of each vertical trim; secure to pillow front, tucking seam allowance under flange. If necessary, trims may be spaced slightly apart.

2 Secure horizontal trims to pillow front as for vertical trims in step 1. Weave trims together; secure remaining ends of trims under flange, trimming any excess length to ¼" (6 mm) seam allowances. Complete pillow as on page 55, steps 6 to 9.

HOW TO SEW A DOUBLE-FLANGE PILLOW WITH DIAGONAL TRIM

MATERIALS

- Solid-color or reversible fabric for the pillow front and pillow back, including the flange, yardage depending on size of project; for 14" (35.5 cm) pillow form and 2½" (6.5 cm) flange, you will need ¾ yd. (0.7 m) of 54" (137 cm) fabric.

- Trims, such as ribbons.

- Pillow form in desired size.

- Polyester fiberfill, for filling out corners.

CUTTING DIRECTIONS

Cut pillow front and pillow back as on page 54.

1 Follow steps 1 to 4 on page 54. Plan the placement of trims. Cut the trims to the lengths needed, allowing ¼" (6 mm) seam allowances.

2 Secure trims to pillow front with glue stick, tucking raw edges under flange. Stitch in place along edges of the trims. Complete pillow as on page 55, steps 6 to 9.

HOW TO SEW A DOUBLE-FLANGE PILLOW WITH BRAID TRIM

MATERIALS

- Fabric for pillow front and pillow back, including flange, yardage depending on size of project; for 14" (35.5 cm) pillow form and 2½" (6.5 cm) flange, you will need ¾ yd. (0.7 m) of 54" (137 cm) fabric.

- Decorative trim, such as braid, for the inner edge of flange, length equal to perimeter of pillow form plus 2" (5 cm).

- Pillow form in desired size.

- Polyester fiberfill, for filling out corners.

CUTTING DIRECTIONS

Cut pillow front and pillow back as on page 54.

1 Press flange and miter corners on *both* pillow front and pillow back as on page 55, step 6. Mark finished width of flange on unmitered side of pillow front, using chalk.

2 Pin braid to pillow front, with outer edge of braid along marked lines; miter braid at corners by folding it at an angle. Fold end of braid diagonally at final corner; trim excess. Edgestitch along inner edge of braid.

3 Pin pillow front and pillow back together with mitered sides facing. Edgestitch along outer edge of braid, leaving an opening for inserting pillow form; hand-stitch mitered corners in place.

4 Insert the pillow form; push fiberfill into the corners of the pillow as necessary to fill out the pillow. Pin the opening closed; complete stitching on outer edge of braid.

HOW TO SEW A DOUBLE-FLANGE PILLOW WITH A PIECED INSERT

MATERIALS

- Fabric for pillow front and pillow back, including flange, yardage depending on size of project; for 14" (35.5 cm) pillow form and 2½" (6.5 cm) flange, you will need ¾ yd. (0.7 m) of 54" (137 cm) fabric.
- Scraps of several fabrics, for pieced insert.
- Pillow form in desired size.
- Polyester fiberfill, of filling out corners.

CUTTING DIRECTIONS

Cut pillow front and pillow back as on page 54.

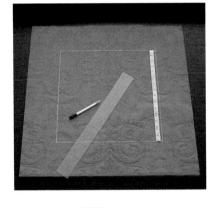

1 Mark square or rectangle, 1" (2.5 cm) larger than pillow form, on wrong side of the pillow front, centering it on the fabric.

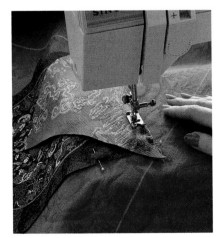

2 Cut a patch of fabric, and place in center or corner of marked area; pin in place. Place a second patch on the first patch, right sides together, aligning one edge. Stitch ¼" (6 mm) seam along aligned edges.

3 Flip the second patch right side up; press. Pin in place. Continue to attach patches until marked area is covered.

4 Sew pillow as on pages 54 and 55, omitting step 5.

For a unique accent, create a pillow from men's discarded suits. Nestled among traditional pillows, a haberdashery pillow adds an unexpected touch of whimsy. The instructions opposite are for a trapezoid-shaped pillow about 16" (40.5 cm) high.

Old suits are readily available at secondhand stores or garage sales. Look for jackets with interesting details. Pockets, buttonholes, and manufacturer's labels add interest to the pillow. Do not overlook lining fabrics and lining details. From the suit pants, welted back pockets, portions of the waistband, and the fly front can be used. A necktie may also be used as an accent.

MATERIALS

- Men's suit coat; suit pants or necktie, optional.
- Muslin, for underlining.
- Purchased welting, if desired.
- Lightweight paper, for pattern.
- Polyester fiberfill.

HOW TO MAKE A HABERDASHERY PILLOW

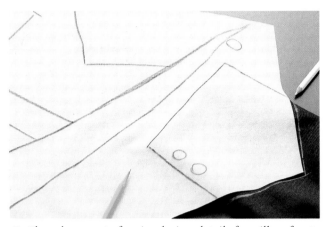

1 Draw 18½" (47.3 cm) line on paper; draw a parallel 9" (23 cm) line centered 17" (43 cm) below first line. Draw connecting lines to make pattern, which includes ½" (1.3 cm) seam allowances. Cut two underlining pieces from muslin, using pattern.

2 Plan placement of major design details for pillow front, such as lapels and pockets, by placing muslin over the garment; mark garment with chalk, and trace design details onto muslin.

3 Cut design pieces from garment, adding ½" (1.3 cm) seam allowances. Cut pieces from the outer layer of the garment only; this allows you to use the lining details for other areas of pillow.

4 Plan placement of smaller pieces, incorporating details such as lining pockets and garment labels. Cut pieces, adding ½" (1.3 cm) seam allowances.

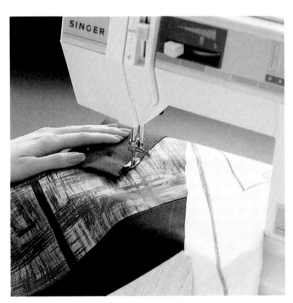

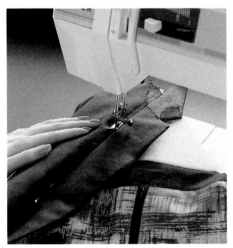

5 Arrange fabric pieces in desired placement; set aside the lapel piece. Stitch remaining pieces to the underlining, using flip-and-stitch and edgestitch methods on page 62. If desired, smaller pieces may be seamed together into larger units before securing them to the underlining.

6 Attach lapel piece by stitching under the lapel, about ¼" (6 mm) from the roll line.

(Continued)

FROM FABRIC & LEATHER

7 Repeat steps 2 to 5 on page 61 for pillow back. Baste around outer edges of the pillow front, within ½" (1.3 cm) seam allowances of muslin underlining; repeat for pillow back. From both pieces, trim excess fabric that extends beyond raw edges of the underlining.

8 Baste welting, if desired, to the pillow front, along one or more seams; tape ends of welting into seam allowance.

9 Pin pillow front to pillow back, right sides together. Stitch ½" (1.3 cm) seam around pillow, leaving opening on one side for turning.

10 Turn pillow right side out, pulling out corners. Press under seam allowances of opening. Stuff the pillow with fiberfill. Slipstitch or edgestitch opening closed.

TIPS FOR JOINING DESIGN PIECES

1 **Stitch-and-flip method.** Apply any garment pieces that have raw edges by placing one piece on muslin underlining; pin in place. Place a second piece on the first piece, right sides together, aligning raw edges. Stitch ½" (1.3 cm) from aligned edges.

2 Flip top garment piece right side up; press. Pin in place. Continue attaching pieces, pressing under ½" (1.3 cm) seam allowance on any raw edges that will not be covered by another piece.

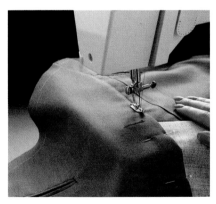

Edgestitch method. Apply any pieces that have finished edges, such as the garment front edge, by stitching them to the muslin underlining close to the finished edge of each piece.

MORE IDEAS FOR HABERDASHERY PILLOWS

Men's shirt is used for the haberdashery pillow, above left, with a necktie added for an accent of color. Men's suit trousers are used for the rectangular pillow, above right. Details include the welted back pocket, the fly front, and the pants cuffs; suspenders were also added.

School band uniform, a memento of school activities, makes a unique haberdashery pillow.

HARDANGER
EMBROIDERY

Hardanger embroidery, with its geometric designs, blends well with most decorating schemes. Hardanger designs are easy to follow and to adapt. Most designs can be stitched by following a close-up photograph.

The embroidery is worked on 22-count Hardanger fabric. This basket-weave fabric is composed of a pattern of squares; each square is made of two strands. Traditionally, pieces were stitched on white fabric with white thread; however, variations combine different colors of fabric and thread.

Learning a few basic Hardanger stitch patterns enables you to create a variety of pieces. You may want to practice the stitches on a small sample before you begin a project. The Hardanger embroidery shown here illustrates various stitch patterns. The finished piece measures 8½" (21.8 cm) square, a suitable size for a first project.

The satin-stitch block is the primary stitch pattern; each block consists of five stitches over four fabric squares. The blocks can be stitched in a variety of patterns, such as a staircase effect or motifs with cutwork. The buttonhole stitch, a variation of the satin-stitch block, forms the edging for many projects. The star motif is also a satin-stitch block variation. Cutwork blocks are stitched using wrapping and web stitches. Satin-stitch blocks, buttonhole stitches, and star motifs are worked

using #5 pearl cotton and a size 22 tapestry needle. Work the wrapping and web stitches for cutwork blocks using #8 pearl cotton and a size 24 tapestry needle.

MATERIALS

- 22-count cotton Hardanger fabric.
- Pearl cotton, #5 and #8.
- Tapestry needles, sizes 22 and 24.
- Sharp, fine-pointed scissors.

TIPS FOR WORKING HARDANGER EMBROIDERY

Practice the stitches, using a contrasting thread, before starting a project.

Check your work often to make sure blocks are properly aligned with the weave of the fabric.

Leave 3" (7.5 cm) thread tails, securing them by weaving the ends under completed stitches on the wrong side of the piece.

Clip threads, rather than carry them; the wrong side of the piece should appear as neat as the right side.

Cut fabric for cutwork by cutting only on the side where the stitches have entered the fabric; never cut parallel to a satin-stitch block.

Hardanger stitch patterns *include cutwork motifs* **(a),** *satin-stitch blocks* **(b),** *star motifs* **(c),** *and buttonhole stitches* **(d).** *The stitches are worked counting the fabric squares, according to a close-up photograph.*

HOW TO STITCH THE HARDANGER SAMPLER PROJECT

1 Cut one 12" (30.5 cm) square of fabric, folding it in quarters to find center of fabric; finger-press. Stitch the center motif of satin-stitch blocks (opposite), starting at a corner about 2½" (6.5 cm) from the center.

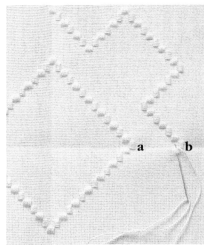

2 Stitch the outer satin-stitch block design; there are 28 squares between the corner block of the center motif **(a)** and the corresponding block of the outer design **(b).** Check work frequently to see that blocks are correctly aligned with the weave of the fabric.

3 Finish design by stitching the outer row of buttonhole stitches, opposite.

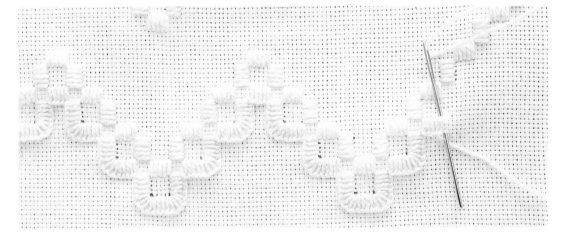

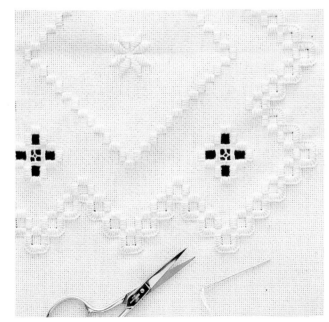

4 Stitch the center star motif (page 69). Stitch cutwork motifs (page 68), using wrapping stitch; add web stitch to center of each cutwork block, if desired.

5 Finish the edges of the Hardanger project as on page 69.

HOW TO MAKE SATIN-STITCH BLOCKS

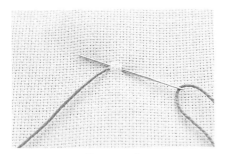

1 Bring needle up and count over four squares; insert the needle, bringing the needle out one square above where thread entered fabric.

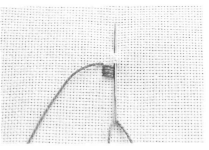

2 Stitch to complete first five-stitch block; on fifth stitch, pivot needle and bring needle up four squares away.

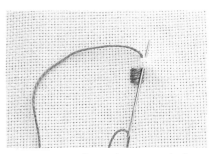

3 Insert needle in the corner hole of previous block to make first stitch of second block.

4 Complete five stitches for the second block; turn second corner by bringing needle up in same hole as last stitch.

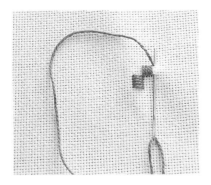

5 Repeat from step 1 for the desired number of satin-stitch blocks, turning corners for desired design.

HOW TO MAKE BUTTONHOLE STITCHES

1 Bring needle up four squares from satin-stitch block. Insert at corner of block and bring out at thread entry, with thread looped under needle. Stitch four additional parallel stitches, looping thread under needle each time.

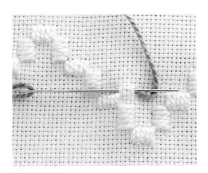

2 Stitch three diagonal stitches, using the corner hole of the fifth parallel stitch for each diagonal stitch; this forms rounded, outside corner.

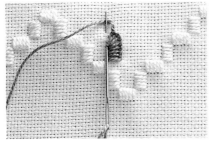

3 Stitch the first parallel stitch of the second block, using the same corner hole.

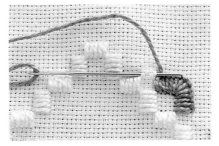

4 Stitch five stitches of second block; at completion of fifth stitch, pivot needle, and stitch across four squares, bringing it up in corner hole of the fifth stitch; this will become the inside corner.

5 Repeat from step 1 for desired number of buttonhole stitches, turning outside and inside corners for desired design. When you run out of thread, start using a new length of thread at an inside corner.

HOW TO MAKE A CUTWORK MOTIF

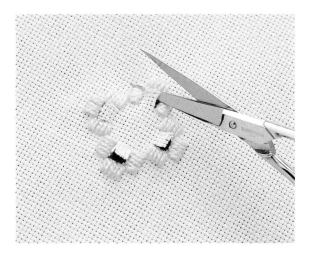

1 **Wrapping stitch.** Stitch a motif of 12 satin-stitch blocks. Carefully cut the fabric as shown; fabric is cut only on the side where the stitches have entered the fabric, never parallel to a satin-stitch block.

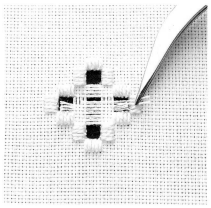

2 Remove all clipped threads from the fabric.

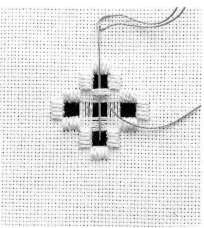

3 Secure thread on wrong side of fabric, and bring needle up through middle of the four unwoven fabric threads. Bring needle around one side and up through the middle.

4 Bring needle around the opposite side and up through the middle.

5 Continue wrapping thread in a figure-eight pattern, pulling each stitch tightly. At completion of first bar, bring needle up through middle of next bar, and repeat to wrap all four sides; if web is desired, wrap one-half of the fourth side.

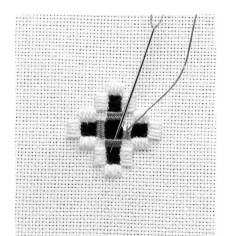

1 **Web stitch.** Follow steps 1 to 5, above, wrapping one-half of the fourth side; insert needle up through center of adjacent bar, creating first web section.

2 Insert needle under web section, then up into next bar.

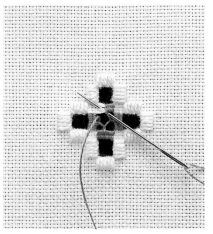

3 Repeat at third bar. Complete the web by bringing needle over and around first web section. Insert needle up into center of uncompleted bar; finish wrapping the bar.

HOW TO MAKE A STAR MOTIF

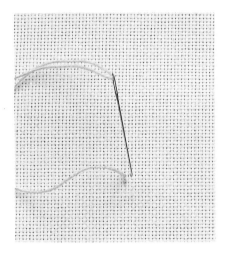

1 Locate center hole for star (as indicated by dot), and count up two squares; bring needle up. Work first satin stitch over two squares.

2 Stitch four additional stitches, increasing the length of each stitch on the right side by one square; fifth stitch covers six squares.

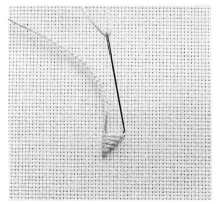

3 Work next stitch by decreasing length on left side by one stitch; stitch remains parallel with previous stitch on the right side.

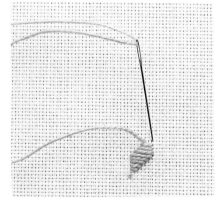

4 Stitch three additional stitches, decreasing the length of each stitch on left side by one square; ninth stitch covers two squares.

5 Insert needle under stitches on wrong side; continue to make eight spokes, working from center out; adjoining spokes share holes. Star is worked in mirror-image pairs.

HOW TO FINISH THE EDGES OF A HARDANGER PROJECT

1 Machine-stitch around the border of the design, stitching just inside the ridge of the buttonhole stitch; use short stitch length and lightweight matching thread. (Contrasting thread was used to show detail.)

2 Trim as close as possible to buttonhole edge, using sharp scissors and taking care not to clip the pearl cotton thread.

MORE IDEAS FOR HARDANGER EMBROIDERY

Placemat, *adapted from an heirloom Hardanger design, is worked on a 16" × 20" (40.5 × 51 cm) rectangle of fabric; the finished size is 12¼" × 16" (31.2 × 40.5 cm). The design consists of satin-stitch blocks, buttonhole stitches, and half-star motifs. Cutwork has been done on the inner satin-stitch blocks, as on page 68. Work the design, counting squares in the fabric and the stitches in the actual-size photograph below.*

Framed doily is mounted on a dark background to highlight the cutwork. Worked on an 11" × 15" (28 × 38 cm) rectangle of fabric, the finished size is 7½" × 11½" (19.3 × 29.3 cm). The design consists of satin-stitch blocks, buttonhole stitches, and cutwork and star motifs. Work the design, counting the fabric squares and stitches in the actual-size photograph below.

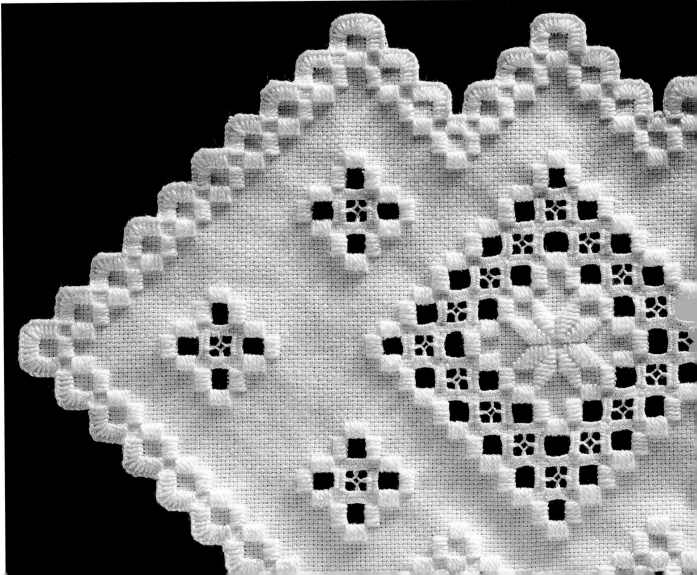

YARN-TRIMMED
RUGS

Add colorful detailing to inexpensive, purchased rag rugs with bits of yarn. Concentrate the yarn embellishments at the ends of the rug to create a border, or scatter them throughout the entire rug. As shown opposite, rugs may be trimmed by stitching the yarn into the rug with a simple running stitch (top), weaving it under the rug's warp threads (bottom), or by combining the two techniques (middle).

MATERIALS

- Purchased rag rug.
- Yarn in desired colors.
- Large-eyed yarn needle.

HOW TO EMBELLISH A RUG WITH WOVEN YARNS

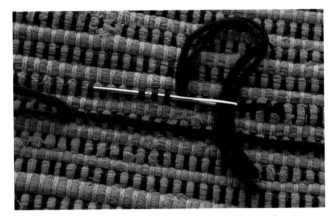

1 Thread needle and secure yarn as in step 1, below. Working from side to side across the rug, run needle under warp threads of rug.

2 Leave 1" (2.5 cm) tails of yarn at end of row, if tufted look is desired. Or secure the end of the yarn as in step 3, below.

HOW TO EMBELLISH A RUG WITH RUNNING STITCHES

1 Fold length of yarn in half; thread ends into needle. Working from top of rug, take a small stitch down and up; pull needle through the loop to secure yarn.

2 Sew running stitches, about ½" (1.3 cm) long. If solid row of stitches is desired, repeat running stitches in opposite direction, sewing between previous stitches.

3 Secure stitches at end of row by taking two or three small stitches; conceal end of the yarn by running needle between the rows of the rug.

Primitive rug hooking is a classic American craft used to make rugs, wall hangings, and pillows. Strips of wool are pulled through a foundation fabric to create a design or picture. The primitive style of hooking, with its simple designs in ¼" (6 mm) wool strips, is easier to master than hooking with narrower strips for more complex designs.

Supplies for rug hooking are minimal and are available at fiber-art stores and through mail-order suppliers. The wool strips may be cut from remnants, discarded garments, or, when necessary, from new pieces of fabric; hand-dyed, color-gradated wool fabrics are also available. To create the muted colors and aged appearance often seen in primitive hooked rugs, the wool fabrics may be simmered in a diluted ammonia solution, a process often referred to as *undyeing* (right).

Cotton monk's cloth is used for the foundation; this fabric is sturdy, flexible, and easy to work with. Cotton twill tape is stitched to the edges of the monk's cloth to prevent raveling during the hooking process; then this same tape is turned under to bind the edges of the completed rug.

In order to achieve even rows of hooked loops, stretch the foundation fabric taut in a frame. A large quilting hoop works well for most small pieces; replace the screw on the outer hoop with a longer screw, if necessary, to allow for additional expansion. Specialized rug-hooking frames, which provide a comfortable working surface, are also available.

Inspiration for designs can come from many sources. Traditional quilt block designs are easily adapted to rug hooking. Patterns from wallpaper, tapestries, and china can also provide design inspiration. Colonial rug designs often featured familiar objects, such as pets, houses, or gardens. Proportion and perspective were not a concern, and the designs often had a whimsical flair.

Start with small, simple designs. A good size for a first project is a wall hanging about 15" (38 cm) square. Select a design that combines various colors and textures. Plaids, herringbones, tweeds, and stripes add texture and create interesting effects. Choose a contrasting background color that allows the design motifs to dominate. In general, the fabric required is about five times the size of the design area.

Prepare the wool fabrics and cotton twill tape by washing them in warm water with a mild detergent, either by hand or by machine in a gentle cycle. Then hang them to dry, or machine dry them. The resulting shrinkage tightens the weave for added strength. Tear or cut the prepared wools into 9" × 12" (23 × 30.5 cm) pieces.

Before starting a project, become familiar with hooking techniques by practicing on a scrap of the foundation fabric, hooking rows in straight lines, curves, and circles. Generally, two threads in the monk's cloth are skipped between the wool loops, and two or three threads are skipped between the rows. If the loops and rows are too close together, the foundation fabric will be stressed and the hooked project will have a lumpy, warped appearance.

Many people prefer to hook the prominent design areas first and any background areas last. You may want to outline a design area by hooking a row of loops around it, then fill in the area with loops. Complete one design area before moving to another.

MATERIALS

- Mediumweight, closely woven fabrics of 100 percent wool.
- Cotton monk's cloth, for foundation.
- Rug hook, in primitive size.
- Rug-hooking frame or wooden quilting hoop.
- Cotton twill tape, 1¼" (3.2 cm) wide, in a color that matches or blends with outer edge of design.
- Heavy-duty cotton thread that matches twill tape.
- Rotary cutter and cutting mat, or sharp scissors.
- Permanent-ink marking pen; transfer pencil; masking tape.
- Mild liquid detergent.

Undyeing is a process that creates muted colors in wool; this gives the wool an aged appearance. Simmer the fabrics for at least 10 minutes in a solution of 1 tsp. (5 mL) ammonia per 1 qt. (0.9 L) water. Rinse the fabric in warm water; then simmer it for 20 minutes in fresh water, with ⅓ c. (79 mL) vinegar added to the water, to set the new color. Rinse the fabric thoroughly; then line dry or machine dry it.

TIPS FOR RUG HOOKING

Mark the colors on the paper pattern, if desired. This is especially helpful for detailed designs.

Strips may be pulled out and rehooked as necessary. Before rehooking, lightly scratch the foundation with your finger to restore the even weave of the fabric.

Vary the direction of the rows within each design area to add a textural effect. This is also used to add interest to large background areas.

Hook at least two rows parallel to and as close as possible to the binding; this will straighten and secure the finished piece.

HOW TO PREPARE THE FOUNDATION

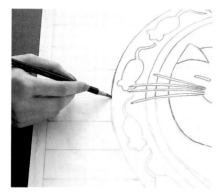

1 Trace design of rug in actual size on a lightweight sheet of paper, allowing for some background area around design motifs.

2 Cut the foundation fabric at least 8" (20.5 cm) larger than finished rug size; fold masking tape around raw edges to prevent raveling. Center finished rug size on foundation; mark, using a permanent-ink marking pen and following grainline of fabric.

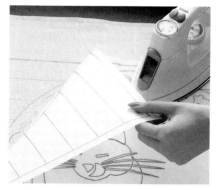

3 Trace the design onto back side of paper pattern, using a transfer pencil. Transfer design to foundation fabric, following the manufacturer's directions, making sure design is aligned with marked lines on the foundation.

4 Fold back ½" (1.3 cm) at end of prewashed twill tape. Stitch outer edge of twill tape to right side of the foundation fabric, with the outer edge positioned just inside marked lines and with folded end of tape at middle of one side; pivot at corners. Trim excess tape, overlapping ends ¾" (2 cm).

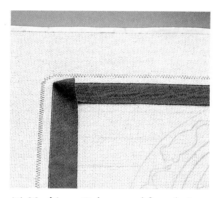

5 Machine-stitch around foundation fabric, using zigzag stitch, ½" (1.3 cm) outside previous stitching; at corners, stitch diagonally as shown. This machine stitching strengthens the finished rug.

6 Fold back twill tape; hand-baste to foundation. At corners, pull twill tape away from design area with stitches.

HOW TO PREPARE THE WOOL

1 Wash wool fabric in warm water with a mild detergent, washing it by hand or by machine in the gentle cycle; line dry or machine dry. Tear or cut wool into 9" × 12" (23 × 30.5 cm) pieces.

2 Cut several lengthwise strips, ¼" (6 mm) wide, from fabric pieces, taking care to follow grainline of fabric. Cut limited amounts as needed, as you hook the rug.

HOW TO HOOK A RUG

1 Secure foundation in a frame or hoop; fabric should be very taut.

2 Hold rug hook in palm of hand, above design, with hook turned up. Hold wool strip between thumb and forefinger of opposite hand; this hand will be held beneath the frame and will guide wool strip, making sure it does not twist.

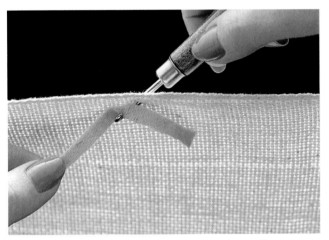

3 Push rug hook down through foundation, and catch the wool strip in hook. Pull end of wool strip to right side, to a height of about 1" (2.5 cm).

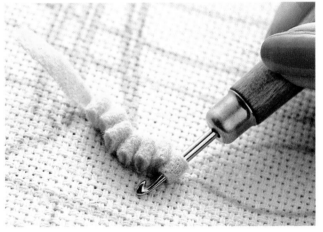

4 Continue hooking wool strip, skipping about two squares in foundation between each insertion of rug hook; pull wool loops to a height of about ¼" (6 mm). Evenly space loops, with no gaps between them, and do not twist wool strip.

5 Allow end of wool strip to extend above foundation on right side; reinsert rug hook in same opening to begin hooking second strip.

6 Clip ends of wool strips even with loops when each design area is completed, taking care not to clip loops.

HOW TO FINISH THE EDGES OF A HOOKED RUG

1 Remove hand basting from twill tape. Trim excess foundation fabric just beyond zigzag stitching.

2 Fold twill tape to underside of rug, mitering the corners; pin in place.

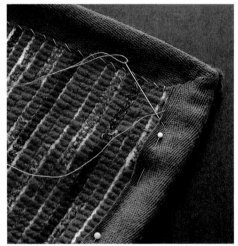

3 Hand-stitch twill tape in place, catching stitches in foundation fabric only. Stitch overlapped ends of tape together, and stitch along mitered corners.

4 Place the rug face down on a clean, flat ironing surface; cover with a dampened towel, and steam press. If shape of rug is distorted, gently straighten or ease it into shape. Allow rug to dry for 24 hours.

5 Make casing for wall hanging, if desired, by hand-stitching twill tape ¼" (6 mm) from upper and lower edges of rug. End the upper casing 1" (2.5 cm) from sides of rug.

6 Insert a metal rod of ¼" or ⅜" (6 mm or 1 cm) diameter into each casing. Stitch ends of lower casing closed. Hang rug on wall by supporting rod on nails.

MORE IDEAS FOR HOOKED RUGS

Traditional design is hooked with a background of subtle color variation. When using a hooked rug on a hardwood or tile floor, place a thin rubber pad under the rug.

Child's drawing, enlarged on a photocopy machine, is used for the design of this pillow. Wool border strips, instead of the usual twill-tape binding, are stitched to the edges of the foundation fabric.

Quilt design, hooked in jewel-tone colors, is inspired by an Amish quilt.

LEATHER
ACCESSORIES

Make a variety of leather accessories, including no-sew laced pillows, custom-sized picture frames, and sturdy baskets. If vegetable-tanned leather is used, the accessories may be stained or personalized with stamped designs.

For laced pillows, select soft, supple leather or suede; a synthetic leather or suede may also be used. For baskets, use a stiff leather, about ⅛" (3 mm) thick, that will provide sufficient support for the sides and handle. For the laced picture frames, made by lacing three layers of leather together, use a stiff leather for the frame back and stand, to provide the proper support; a softer, lightweight leather or suede may be used for the frame front.

The leather skins and any necessary supplies are available at leather craft and supply stores. For the laced edges of pillows and picture frames and the ties on leather baskets, leather and suede lacing is available in various widths. To determine the amount of lacing needed for a laced pillow, allow about three times the distance to be laced, plus 1¼ yd. (1.15 m) for knotted ends. For a picture frame, allow about four times the distance around the outside of the frame. For the ties on a leather basket, 2 yd. (1.85 m) of lacing is used.

A punch tool and mallet are used to make lacing holes in leather quickly and easily. Punch tools are available in many sizes; a size 4, or ⁵⁄₃₂" (3.8 mm), punch tool will work for most lacing. Saddle-stamping tools, available in a variety of designs, are used for making stamped designs on heavyweight vegetable-tanned leather. When punching and stamping leather, work on a hard, smooth surface, such as a sturdy workbench or a piece of firm Masonite® or marble.

For aligning stamped designs, a placement line may be lightly scored on the leather with your fingernail. Do not draw the line with a pencil, because pencil markings often cannot be removed without marring the leather. A pencil may be used for marking lacing holes that will be punched out of the leather.

Special leather stains are available in several shades. They not only change the color of a vegetable-tanned leather, they also bring out the grain and enhance any stamped designs. Before applying stain to a project, test it on a scrap of the leather you will be using. If stain is being applied to a lightweight leather, some shrinkage may occur. Leather finishes are also available; they provide a durable, water-repellent finish and a soft luster.

MATERIALS

- Leather.
- Leather lacing.
- Leather round-drive punch tool, in size appropriate for lacing; a size 4, or ⁵⁄₃₂", will work for most leather lacing.
- Two-pronged leather-lacing needle.
- Mallet, of wood, rubber, or rawhide.
- Mat knife or rotary cutter; metal straightedge.
- Pillow form, in desired size, for pillow.
- Decorative beads, optional, for pillow.
- Cardboard, optional, for frame.
- Saddle-stamping tools, for stamped designs.
- Leather stain, optional.
- Leather finish.

Leather accessories, *such as a laced pillow and frame and a stamped basket, give a room the rustic look of a country lodge.*

HOW TO MAKE A LACED LEATHER PILLOW

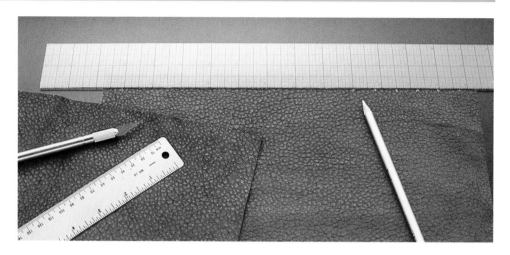

1 Cut the pillow front and pillow back from leather, using a metal straightedge and a mat knife or rotary cutter, cutting pieces 1" (2.5 cm) wider and longer than pillow form. Using chalk or lead pencil, mark placement for lacing holes on top side of pillow front, ⅝" (1.5 cm) from the edges; position a hole at each corner and at intervals of ¾" to 1" (2 to 2.5 cm).

2 Punch holes for lacing in pillow front, using punch tool and mallet. Place the pillow front on pillow back, top sides together. Using pillow front as a guide, mark holes on top side of pillow back. Punch holes.

3 Cut a length of lacing equal to three times the length of first side to be laced plus 12" (30.5 cm). Using mat knife, trim end of lacing to a point.

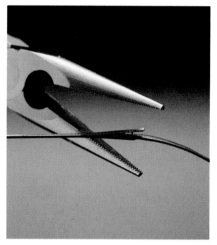

4 Open the leather needle at the spring end; insert the lacing with top side of lacing against the prongs. Using needlenose pliers, squeeze the needle so prongs pierce lacing.

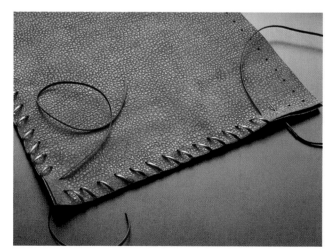

5 Place pillow front on pillow back, top sides facing out. Using whipstitch, lace the first side; leave about 6" (15 cm) tails at ends. Repeat to lace three sides of pillow.

6 Insert pillow form. Lace the remaining side. Tie ends of lacing at corners. Attach beads, if desired, securing them with overhand knot.

HOW TO MAKE A LEATHER BASKET

1 Cut 12" (30.5 cm) square of paper; fold to divide into fourths, then eighths. Using a compass at folded center point, draw a circle with 5¾" (14.5 cm) radius; cut. Mark placement for lacing holes on folds, ¼" (6 mm) from outer edge.

2 Mark the bottom of basket, and cut from leather with rotary cutter or mat knife, using paper pattern as a guide; transfer markings for holes. Cut 6" × 37" (15 × 94 cm) leather strip for sides. Cut 2" × 24" (5 × 61 cm) leather strip for handle.

3 Mark eight holes, ¼" (6 mm) from lower edge of side piece and 4⅜" (11.2 cm) apart, with the first hole 3" (7.5 cm) from end. Punch holes in the bottom and side piece of the basket at markings.

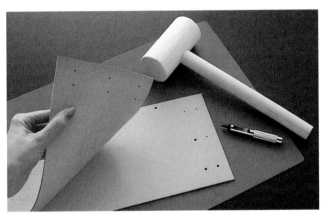

4 Mark three holes, ⅝" (1.5 cm) from short end of side piece, 1" (2.5 cm) from the top, at center, and 1" (2.5 cm) from the bottom. Mark a second row of three holes, ¾" (2 cm) from the first row. Repeat at opposite short end of side piece. Punch holes.

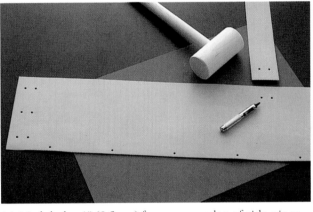

5 Mark holes 1" (2.5 cm) from upper edge of side piece, 18⅛" and 18⅞" (46.3 and 48.2 cm) from one short end; these are used for attaching handle. Mark two holes in handle, 1" (2.5 cm) from short end and ⅝" (1.5 cm) from long edges; repeat at opposite end. Punch holes.

6 Stamp, stain, and finish the leather, if desired (page 85). Overlap short ends of side strip, aligning the holes. Secure side piece at each pair of holes, using 6" (15 cm) lengths of lacing; attach the handle to inside of the basket when securing the upper edge. Attach the handle at other side of the basket, using 6" (15 cm) length of lacing.

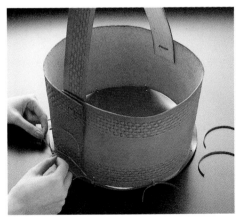

7 Secure the side piece to basket bottom at holes, using 6" (15 cm) lengths of lacing. Trim ends of lacing, if desired.

HOW TO MAKE A LACED LEATHER FRAME

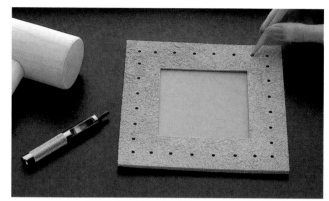

1 Determine size of picture opening; picture can be no more than ¼" (6 mm) wider than opening. To length and width, add 2¾" (7 cm) to allow for 1⅜" (3.5 cm) borders; this is finished size. Cut two pieces of stiff leather equal to the finished size, using mat knife; these will be frame back and stand. Cut a third piece for frame front; this may be cut from leather of a lighter weight. Mark picture opening on frame front; cut.

2 Mark placement for lacing holes on top side of frame front, ½" (1.3 cm) from edges, using pencil or chalk; position a hole at each corner and at regular intervals of about ¾" (2 cm). Punch holes, using a punch tool and a mallet. Place the frame front on the frame stand, top sides together. Using the frame front as a guide, mark holes on the frame stand. Punch holes.

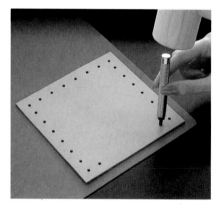

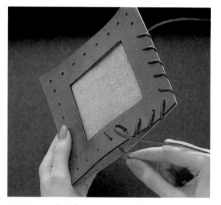

3 Mark and punch holes on frame back; at lower edge, punch only one hole in from each corner hole. This leaves opening for inserting picture. Stamp, stain, and finish the leather, if desired (opposite).

4 Position frame front on back, top sides facing out. Secure lacing to leather needle as on page 82, step 4. Insert needle from back of frame, into hole about one-third the distance from the top; leave tail for knotting ends.

5 Lace the frame together, using whipstitch, along first side and lower edge; at opening on lower edge, lacing is done through frame front only.

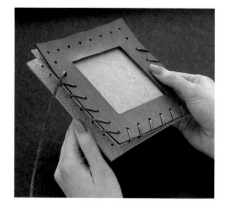

6 Lace the remaining side to hole opposite starting point. Position frame stand against frame back, with top sides facing out.

7 Lace through all layers of frame to attach stand to upper portion of sides and along top edge.

8 Continue lacing around the frame stand only.

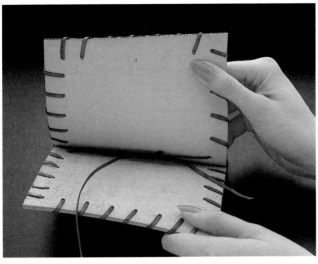

9 Bring ends of lacing across the frame, between frame back and frame stand; tie ends together. Trim tails.

10 Insert the picture into laced frame.

HOW TO STAMP, STAIN & FINISH LEATHER

1 Stamp. Prepare leather by wiping both sides with a dampened sponge; place in plastic bag, and allow to set several hours. Remove leather from bag; allow surface of leather to dry, just until original leather color returns.

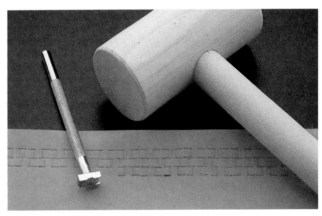

2 Place leather on hard, smooth surface, top side up. Position saddle-stamping tool on leather; pound with mallet until imprint is clear.

Stain. Stamp leather, if desired. Apply a liberal coat of leather stain to leather, using a rag and circular motion; allow to set several minutes. Remove excess stain, using a dampened sponge; if leather is stamped, stain should remain in crevices of stamped design. Allow to dry.

Finish. Apply an even, light coat of leather finish, using dampened sponge; allow to dry. Apply second coat of finish. When dry, buff leather with soft rag.

MORE IDEAS FOR LEATHER ACCESSORIES

Albums and note pads *with leather covers are embellished with twigs and beads, inserted into the lacing.*

Colorful assortment of suedes *is used to make a collection of frames; contrasting black lacing unifies the frames.*

Strips of leather *are pieced together on the diagonal for this pillow front. Overlap the strips, and stitch, using a leather needle. Or glue the strips, using a leather cement.*

Animal skin *is used for the front of a laced pillow. Mark and punch the holes from the back side of the skin.*

Pair of baskets *adds texture to a rustic decorating scheme. The smaller basket is stamped in an all-over design. The larger basket has an added strip of textured leather laced near the top.*

Clocks, Frames,
Ceramics
& More

DECORATIVE FRAMES

Starting with simple frames for pictures or mirrors, you can create frames that are eye-catching conversation pieces. A mix of several frames in various styles can be grouped together for added impact.

For a rustic, woodland look, make twig frames (top left). Or use your creativity to add moss, stones, or other natural materials (pages 94 and 95).

Embellished frames (far left) are quick and easy to make. Any number of items can be glued to frames, including buttons, coins, gemstones, beads, or charms.

Use a glue that will bond to both the frame and the embellishment. Hot glue is suitable for many items, including plastics, twigs, and bark. When gluing metal items, use a glue suitable for metals, such as a jewelry glue. When applying moss, use a wood glue. Because there must be sufficient bonding surface between the frame and the embellishment, a frame with a flat surface usually works best.

Decoupage frames (near left), embellished with cutouts from gift-wrapping paper, can be made in designs from Victorian to whimsical. Prepare the cutout motifs, following the instructions for art plates on page 104. For a quick decoupage finish, use an aerosol glaze. For a thick gloss on frames, use a glaze formulated for a triple-thick, extra-thick, or deep-gloss finish.

HOW TO MAKE A TWIG FRAME

MATERIALS

- Frame with flat surface in a color that matches the twigs.
- Straight twigs that will fit closely together.
- Hot glue gun and glue sticks; utility scissors.

1 Plan twig placement; cut twigs to the desired lengths. Position twigs on frame, arranging them as necessary for a close fit.

2 Secure twigs to one side of frame, applying the hot glue to the twigs. Glue twigs starting at inner edge of frame and working toward outer edge. Continue securing twigs to complete all sides.

HOW TO MAKE AN EMBELLISHED FRAME

MATERIALS

- Frame.
- Wire cutter.
- Embellishments, such as charms, shells, beads, buttons, and coins.
- Glue, appropriate for securing embellishments.

1 Remove any unnecessary hardware, such as button shanks or charm loops, from embellishments, using a wire cutter.

2 Plan placement of the items; for visual interest, consider using an asymmetrical design or extending some items over edge of frame.

3 Secure items with glue; to avoid excess glue, apply it sparingly to back of charm, making sure to cover all flat surfaces that will be in contact with frame.

HOW TO MAKE A DECOUPAGE FRAME

MATERIALS

- Frame.
- Gift-wrapping paper.
- Decoupage medium.
- Small sponge applicator, optional.
- Scissors with fine, sharp blades and points; curved cuticle scissors, for intricate, curved motifs.
- Spray glaze.

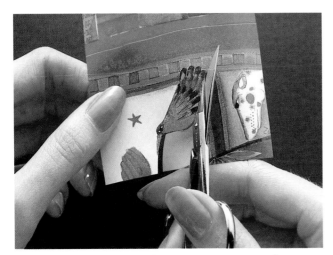

1 Cut out desired motifs from wrapping paper; if using cuticle scissors, cut with curved blades of scissors away from the motif.

2 Plan the placement of the motifs. Apply a thin layer of decoupage medium to back of motif, using sponge applicator or finger; secure to frame, taking care not to tear paper. Wipe any excess decoupage medium from frame.

3 Secure other embellishments, such as faceted stones, taking care not to use excessive amount of decoupage medium; allow to dry overnight.

4 Elevate frame on a piece of scrap wood or a jar. Apply several coats of spray glaze, allowing the glaze to dry between coats.

MORE IDEAS
FOR DECORATIVE FRAMES

Spanish moss and twigs *embellish a mirror with a simple, wide frame.*

Bundled twigs, *tied with raffia, make a woodland frame.*

Buttons and beads *are tied at the corner of a rustic frame. A hole drilled through the frame allows for lacing the items.*

Polished stones *are glued to a frame to complement a nature print.*

Gift card *is cut to make a decorative mat. Use a straightedge and a mat knife to cut an opening for the picture.*

Clocks can be made quickly and easily using decorative ceramic plates or picture frames, as on page 99. Or build a mantel-style clock from wood scraps, as on page 100.

Battery-operated clock movements are available in two types: bezel clock inserts and shaft-style movements. Both types are available at craft stores and from mail-order suppliers.

Bezel clock inserts are fully assembled and are simply inserted into a clock case with a round opening; springs hold the insert in place. Available in a variety of sizes and styles, most inserts require a ¾" (2 cm) mounting depth. Clock cases may be purchased, or you can make your own wooden clock case. If you are making your own, the round opening for the clock insert is easily cut into the wood with a jigsaw.

Shaft-style clock movements are inserted from the back of the mounting surface through a small drilled hole; the hands are then attached to the shaft. Several styles of hands, as well as other clock parts (page 98), are available for use with shaft-style clock movements. Purchase shaft-style movements according to the thickness of the mounting surface; shaft sizes can accommodate various mounting depths, up to ¾" (2 cm).

For shaft-style clocks, use a drill bit that is appropriate for the material you are drilling through. Use a brad-point bit when drilling through acrylic and a ceramic bit for drilling through glass. When drilling acrylic and glass, drill slowly to minimize the risk of cracking. For picture-frame clocks, look for frames that will not interfere with the location of the clock mechanism. You may display the frame on a decorative easel.

Decorative plate *becomes a clock by adding a shaft-style clock movement and a numeral ring.*

Picture frame and a shaft-style movement are used for this clock. Self-adhesive markers add the finishing touch.

Wooden clock case, made from wood scraps, and a bezel insert create a contemporary mantel clock.

Bezel clock inserts (a) are available in various sizes and styles. A bezel insert may be used with a purchased clock case **(b)** or one that you make yourself.

Shaft-style movements (a) allow you to make clocks from plates, picture frames, and other objects up to ¾" (2 cm) in thickness. Several styles of hands **(b)**, markers **(c)**, dials **(d)**, numeral rings **(e)**, and individual numerals **(f)** are available for use with shaft-style movements.

HOW TO MAKE A PLATE OR PICTURE-FRAME CLOCK

MATERIALS

- Picture frame, or ceramic or glass plate.
- Shaft-style clock movement, in appropriate size for thickness of mounting surface.
- Glue gun and glue sticks, if necessary, for drilling glass or ceramic; drill.

- Brad-point drill bit, for drilling acrylic; ceramic drill bit and mineral spirits, for drilling ceramic or glass; bullet-point drill bit, for drilling cardboard frame backing. (Size of bit depends on diameter of threaded portion of clock shaft.)

1 **Picture frame.** Mount decorative paper or picture in frame. Mark the placement of hole for clock shaft on glass. Remove picture and cardboard. Using hot glue and mineral spirits as for ceramic plate, right, drill hole the diameter of clock shaft through glass; use appropriate drill bit, drilling slowly to minimize risk of breakage. Reassemble frame; drill through remaining layers, as shown.

1 **Ceramic or glass plate.** Mark the placement of hole for clock shaft at center of plate. Pour mineral spirits into the plate. For a plate with a flat surface, create a well by applying ring of hot glue to plate; fill the well with mineral spirits. Drill hole the diameter of clock shaft; use ceramic drill bit, drilling slowly to minimize risk of breakage.

2 Mount hanger, if desired, on clock shaft. Place rubber gasket on back of plate or frame. Insert shaft through hole; secure on front of plate with brass washer and hex nut.

3 Attach hour hand; press lightly, taking care not to bend hand. Attach minute hand. Secure hands with a cap nut; or secure with an open nut, and attach second hand. Affix numeral ring or dial markings and numerals.

HOW TO MAKE A MANTEL CLOCK

MATERIALS

- Scraps of 1 × 2 lumber.
- 1 × 8 board, for clock face.
- 3" to 4" (7.5 to 10 cm) bezel clock insert; compass.
- Wood glue; 1½" (3.8 cm) brads; nail set.
- Acrylic paints or wood stain.
- Aerosol acrylic sealer, optional.
- Decorative handle or ornament, for top of clock.
- Jigsaw, with narrow, fine-tooth blade; clamps.

1 Cut one 6" × 7" (15 × 18 cm) wood piece for face of clock from 1 × 8 board; cut with grain of wood along length of piece. Determine placement of clock insert. Mark diameter for back of insert on wood at desired location, using a compass.

2 Cut hole for clock insert just outside marked line, using a jigsaw; this allows ease for inserting clock mechanism. For accurate cutting, use a narrow, fine-tooth jigsaw blade. Check fit of clock insert. Enlarge the hole, if necessary. Set aside clock insert.

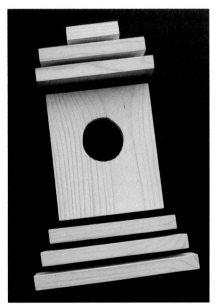

3 Cut 7" (18 cm), 8" (20.5 cm), and 9" (23 cm) lengths from 1 × 2 lumber for the base pieces of clock. Cut 3" (7.5 cm), 6" (15 cm), and 6¾" (17 cm) lengths for top pieces.

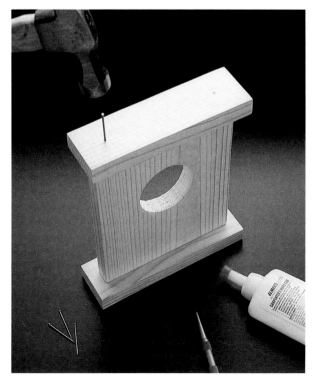

4 Center bottom edge of clock face on top of 7" (18 cm) piece; glue. Secure with 1½" (3.8 cm) brads. Center 6¾" (17 cm) piece on the top edge of clock face; glue. Secure with brads, placing the brads at least 1" (2.5 cm) from ends. Countersink brads, using a nail set.

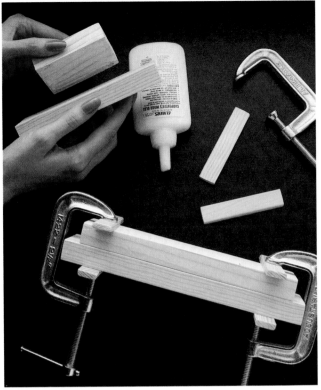

5 Center 8" (20.5 cm) base piece on 9" (23 cm) piece; glue. Clamp and allow to dry. Center 3" (7.5 cm) top piece on 6" (15 cm) piece; glue. Clamp and allow to dry.

6 Glue the base pieces to bottom of clock case. Glue the top pieces to top of clock case.

7 Paint or stain the clock case as desired; paints may be applied using natural sea sponge, as on page 107, steps 8 and 9. Apply aerosol acrylic sealer. Attach handle or ornament to top of clock case.

8 Attach bezel clock insert; rotate the insert to properly align the dial.

Paperweight *is made into a clock with the addition of a mini bezel clock insert. The hole was drilled into the wooden paperweight with a Forstner drill bit.*

Metal frame displays a shaft-style clock as well as a picture cut from a magazine.

Wooden box is turned on its side with the shaft of the clock movement inserted through the bottom of the box. The face of the clock is created from hardware findings.

Wooden building blocks are used with a mini bezel clock insert. Wood glue secures the blocks.

Acrylic picture frame (right) becomes a unique tabletop clock by combining a shaft-style clock movement with ornate hands and a printed geometric insert.

Wooden bookend with a mini bezel clock insert serves a dual purpose.

DECOUPAGE ART PLATES

Transform a clear glass plate into a unique decorative plate, using simple decoupage techniques and motifs cut from gift-wrapping paper. The motifs are glued to the back of the plate with a decoupage medium. For a background with a dimensional effect, paints are then applied, using a sponging technique. Varnish is applied as a sealer over the sponged paint.

For the motifs, select high-quality gift-wrapping papers, often sold in individual sheets; avoid papers that are very light in weight. Designs from greeting cards and antique reproduction prints may also be used for motifs. For best results when working with heavy papers such as greeting cards, reduce the thickness by peeling away one or more layers.

MATERIALS

- Clear glass plate.
- Gift-wrapping paper.
- Decoupage medium; brush or sponge applicator.
- Acrylic paints; small piece of natural sea sponge, for applying paints.
- Scissors with fine, sharp blades and points.
- Curved cuticle scissors, for intricate, curved motifs.
- Aerosol acrylic sealer.
- Sponge or brayer.

1 Cut out the desired motifs from gift-wrapping paper; if using cuticle scissors, cut with curved blades away from motif.

2 Outline paper motifs or highlight the designs, using marking pens, if desired. Seal the ink with aerosol acrylic sealer.

3 Trace the plate on piece of paper; plan placement of motifs. Clean the back of plate thoroughly, using glass cleaner and lint-free rag; place plate face down on table.

4 Apply a thin layer of decoupage medium to the front of center foreground motif, using sponge applicator or finger.

5 Position the motif on back of plate; smooth out bubbles or wrinkles, using a dampened sponge or brayer. Any excess decoupage medium around edges of the motif will not show when the plate is painted.

6 Continue applying motifs, working out from center of plate; if motifs are layered, work from foreground to background. Allow decoupage medium to dry.

7 Apply thin coat of decoupage medium to the back of the motifs as a sealer; allow to dry.

8 Apply the lightest color of acrylic paint, using natural sea sponge; apply sparingly.

9 Apply remaining layers of paint, finishing with darkest color. If desired, paint back of plate a solid color, using an aerosol acrylic paint.

10 Personalize plate with signature and date, using permanent-ink marking pen.

11 Apply light coat of aerosol acrylic sealer; allow sealer to dry. Apply second coat.

Transform plain glazed ceramics into one-of-a-kind accessories, using ceramic paints. These water-based paints, such as Liquitex® Glossies™ and DEKA®-Gloss, provide a durable, scratch-resistant surface. The painted pieces can be heat-hardened in a low-temperature oven to further improve the paint's durability, adhesion, and water resistance.

The easiest ceramics to paint are glazed ceramics that have low-relief decorative motifs. These are available in a variety of pieces, including plates, pitchers, vases, candlesticks, and bowls.

You may also select plain pieces of glazed ceramic, creating your own design to complement other decorative elements in your home. For design and color inspiration, mimic the designs in wallpaper, fabric, or artwork.

Water-based ceramic paints are available in a variety of colors and may be mixed for custom colors. To become familiar with the paints, test them on a small plate before starting a project. The paints vary in transparency, and some are easier to work with if they are thinned. Ceramic paints often result in an uneven coverage; this becomes part of the unique character of each piece. You may

want to spread the paints thinly, allowing the brush marks to show, in order to emphasize the hand-painted quality of the design. When painting raised motifs, thin the paints as necessary to allow the texture of the relief to show.

Use ceramic paints for decorative items only. Although nontoxic, these paints are not recommended for eating or drinking utensils where food will come into contact with the paint. Heat-hardened pieces may be gently washed in cool water with a mild detergent; do not soak the pieces in water. With some paints, the heat-hardened ceramics may be washed in the dishwasher; refer to the manufacturer's label.

MATERIALS

- Water-based ceramic paints.
- Artist's brushes, such as a liner for small areas and a flat shader for larger areas.
- Pallette, such as a plastic lid.
- Fine-point marking pen, tracing paper, graphite paper, and Con-Tact® self-adhesive vinyl, for marking original designs.

Ceramic accessories *may be painted with original designs (above). Or the raised motifs on sculptured ceramics (opposite) may be painted to emphasize the detailing.*

1 Test the consistency of the paint on bottom of item to be painted or on a separate ceramic item. Paint dominant motifs. If desired, mix two or three shades of paint, distributing shades evenly among motifs. Allow to dry.

2 Paint secondary motifs, such as leaves, working with mixed shades of a color, if desired. Allow to dry.

3 Paint any small, detailed areas, such as tendrils or berries, thinning the paint, if necessary, to allow the raised design to show through. Allow to dry.

4 Paint rims or handle, if desired. Allow to dry. Bake finished piece in low-temperature oven, following manufacturer's directions.

HOW TO PAINT ORIGINAL DESIGNS ON CERAMICS

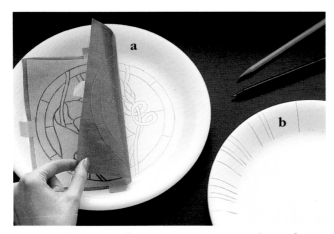

1 Trace design motifs onto tissue paper, and transfer design to ceramic, using carbon or graphite paper **(a).** Or draw designs directly on ceramics, using fine-point marking pen **(b).**

2 Apply self-adhesive vinyl to ceramic item to mask off areas that are to remain white, such as the center area of a plate; this helps in painting smooth, even edges. Use a mat knife to trim vinyl edges.

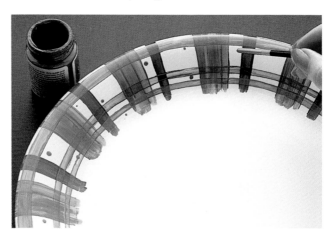

3 Test the consistency of the paint on bottom of item to be painted or on a separate ceramic item. Paint the design areas, one color at a time, allowing the paint to dry before proceeding to the next color; the paint may overlap the vinyl in masked areas.

4 Add any outlining or other small details of the design over previous paint.

5 Remove the self-adhesive vinyl after paint has dried. Bake finished piece in low-temperature oven, following manufacturer's directions.

MOSAIC
ACCESSORIES

The art of mosaic transforms a utilitarian vase into a dramatic piece of artwork. Made from broken or cut tiles separated by sanded grout, each mosaic piece has a unique quality. Tiles can be applied over any surface that is clean, dry, and structurally sound. If the surface is glossy, lightly sand it before applying the tiles.

Ceramic tiles, available in matte and gloss finishes, may be cut into squares or rectangles no smaller than ¾" (2 cm), or into random shapes, then applied to a vase, clay pot, or other accessory. Large tiles are sold individually, and smaller tiles may be purchased in sheets that cover about 1 sq. ft. (30.5 sq. cm); tiles in sheets may be pulled off the mesh backing.

The ceramic tiles are cut into the desired shapes and sizes with a tile cutter. The surface of the tile is first scored with the tool's cutting wheel. Then the tile is broken along the scored line by pressing the breaking wings of the cutter against the tile.

Several types of tile cutters are available. A hand cutter may be used for cutting the softer tiles. With this cutter, you will need to measure the cutting lines and mark them on the tile with a marking pen; the markings can be wiped off with a dampened rag after the tile is cut.

For tiles that are so hard they cannot be cut successfully with a hand cutter, use a large commercial-type cutter, which may be borrowed or rented from a tile store. The commercial-type cutter is more convenient for cutting tiles into exact dimensions without having to mark the cutting lines. Set the guide on the cutter for the desired dimension; then lay the tile on the cutter against the guide. You will still need a hand cutter to break the tiles, because the breaking wings on a commercial-type cutter are too wide to break the small pieces necessary for making mosaic designs.

To cut random-shaped pieces of tile, use the breaking wings of a hand cutter without scoring the tile. Grip the tile against the breaking wings, and squeeze firmly. When using a hand cutter, you may want to break the tiles inside a paper bag, as a safety precaution and to help keep the work area clean.

Plan the mosaic design before beginning. Measure the space on the vase or pot to determine the size of the tiles to be cut. If you want to work in rows, determine the number of rows that will fit, planning to space the tiles ⅛" to ¼" (3 to 6 mm) apart. Keep in mind that the spacing between the tiles does not have to be exact; some irregularity adds to the unique character of the piece.

Tile cutters include a commercial-type cutter **(a)** for cutting hard tiles and a hand cutter **(b)** for cutting softer tiles.

MATERIALS

- Vase, clay pot, or other accessory.
- Ceramic tiles in matte or gloss finish; shards of pottery may be substituted.
- Ceramic adhesive or multipurpose household adhesive, such as Liquid Nails®.
- Tile cutter.
- Sanded tile grout and grout float.
- Plastic ice-cream bucket; rubber gloves.
- Cellulose sponge.
- Coarse nylon sponge.
- Self-adhesive felt pad, for bottom of vase or pot.
- Grout sealer, optional.

HOW TO MAKE A MOSAIC VASE

1 Set the guide on commercial-type tile cutter to desired width. If using a hand cutter, mark cutting line on tile. Score tile with cutting wheel by pulling wheel firmly and slowly across tile.

2 Break tile along the scored line with a hand cutter, centering scored line between breaking wings. Press with slow, steady motion.

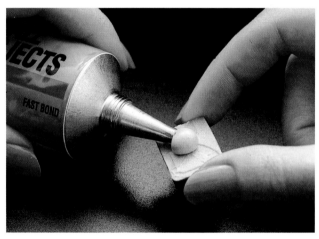

3 Squeeze a pea-size bead of adhesive onto the wrong side of the tile.

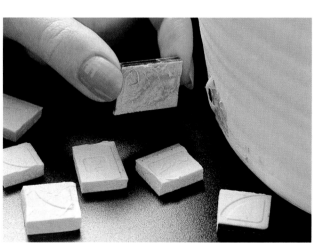

4 Press the tile onto the clay vase or pot in the desired location, beginning with narrowest portion of vase or pot. For faster setting, pull tile away from vase; air dry for 5 to 8 minutes.

5 Continue applying tiles as in step 4. Allow adhesive to cure for 16 to 24 hours, until the tiles have firmly set.

7 Apply grout by drawing grout float across tiles at a slight angle to the surface, forcing the grout into spaces between tiles; wear rubber gloves. Use the short side of the grout float for small projects, the longer side for large projects. Go over each area two or three times, making sure grout is worked in thoroughly, filling in all gaps and air holes.

6 Prepare the sanded grout according to the manufacturer's directions.

8 Remove the excess grout from tiles, using a dampened cellulose sponge, after about 20 minutes or when grout is firm, but not completely hardened; rub dampened sponge in circular motion over tiles.

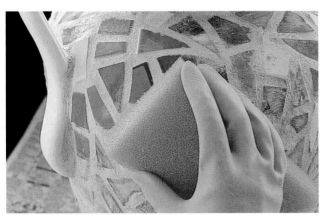

9 Rub the tiles with a coarse nylon sponge to remove the haze, 2 or 3 hours after the first cleaning was done with dampened cellulose sponge.

10 Paint inside of vase, or any areas not covered with mosaic, with grout that has been diluted with water to a thin consistency. Polish the tiles with a clean, dry cloth. Apply grout sealer, if desired.

Mosaic tabletop *transforms this small table into a unique accent piece. Apply the tiles to an existing tabletop or to a top cut from plywood.*

Plaster pedestal *is decorated with tiles. The scrollwork areas of the pedestal are painted with sanded grout that has been thinned with water.*

Shallow bowl *is created by covering a terra-cotta saucer with mosaic tiles inside and out.*

Shards of pottery *have been substituted for tiles, for a more irregular piece of artwork.*

The warm glow of candles makes a room inviting. A wide array of candles is available, from slender tapers to chunky pillars.

For a romantic touch, use delicate French ribbon to add bows and streamers to candles. Or secure embellishments to a chimney-style candle with floral adhesive or rubber bands, which are then concealed with ribbon or raffia.

Candles can be quickly embellished with decorative nail heads. To avoid excessive cracking, use nail heads with prongs not longer than ⅛" (3 mm) and press the prongs gently into the candle.

Clusters of candles *create a simple centerpiece with impact. Opposite, the pillar candles are enhanced with French ribbons and studded with decorative nail heads.*

Chimney-style candles *can be surrounded by sprigs of holly and evergreen. Or twigs can be tied around the chimney with raffia.*

Floating candles *and smooth glass stones in a clear, heavy dish suggest the tranquility of a woodland pool.*

JAR-IN-A-JAR CANDLES

Recycle jars to make decorative containers for votive candles. A small jar containing the votive candle is placed inside a larger jar, and the space between them is filled with embellishments. When lit, the candle softly illuminates the embellishments.

A variety of looks can be achieved, using marbles, pods, leaves, dried flowers, colored pasta, potpourri, and shells. For a woodland look, wrap the inner jar with dried naturals, such as lavender, and place it on a piece of floral foam that has been covered with moss.

When filling the space between the jars with dense items, use an inner jar that is only slightly smaller than the outer jar and do not place the items too closely together. If the space between the jars is too wide or too solidly filled, the light from the candle will not glow through the embellishments.

MATERIALS

- Jars.
- Votive candle.
- Floral adhesive.
- Embellishments as desired.
- Rubber band, if needed for securing embellishments.
- Floral foam and sheet moss, if desired.
- Ribbon or raffia, if desired.

Clear glass marbles (above) or preserved autumn leaves and dried naturals (opposite) are used for creative jar-in-a-jar candles.

TIPS FOR MAKING JAR-IN-A-JAR CANDLES

Secure jars with floral adhesive. Stack two inner jars, if necessary, to achieve desired height.

Secure items such as leaves or stems around jar, using rubber band; conceal rubber band with ribbon or raffia bow.

Conceal threaded tops of jars with ribbon, if desired.

SEASONAL ARRANGEMENTS

For a versatile floral arrangement that can be used as a centerpiece or atop an armoire, prepare a basketful of silk greenery, accenting it with flowers, berries, or dried naturals that reflect the season. Change the accents as the seasons change for a new look. For a fast and easy arrangement, select full clusters of silk greens with long, flexible stems that can be arranged for a natural appearance.

MATERIALS

- Basket or other desired container.
- Silk greens.
- Floral Styrofoam®.
- Floral adhesive clay.
- Spanish moss.
- Spring embellishments, such as silk irises and crocuses and pussy-willow stems.
- Summer embellishments, such as silk daisies, latex fruit, and branches.
- Fall embellishments, such as honeysuckle vines, preserved autumn leaves, and dried pods.
- Winter embellishments, such as artificial greens, pinecones, and assorted berries.

Spring arrangement *(opposite) features the fresh look of irises, crocuses, and pussy willows. Insert the flowers, clustering each variety and varying the height of the stems. For added texture, insert several pussy-willow stems, varying the height.*

Summer arrangement *(right) is a bright accent for a sunny room. Insert stems of daisies, varying the height of the stems. For added texture, insert latex fruit and several branches, varying the height.*

Autumn arrangement *(below, left) has the warm colors of the season. Tuck short lengths of honeysuckle vine among the greens. Insert several stems of bittersweet and autumn leaves.*

Winter arrangement *(below, right) uses seasonal embellishments that outlast the Christmas holiday. Insert artificial evergreens, pinecones, and assorted berries.*

HOW TO MAKE A SEASONAL ARRANGEMENT

1 Cut the floral Styrofoam to fit the basket snugly; top of foam should be slightly lower than top of basket. Secure the foam, if necessary, using floral adhesive clay. Cover the foam with Spanish moss.

2 Insert stems of greens into the foam. Shape individual stems into soft curves, bending ends of tendrils for natural appearance. Add seasonal embellishments.

WIRE MESH SACHETS

Potpourri sachets add a refreshing scent to any room and serve as decorative accents. For a unique, textural sachet, create one from aluminum window screening. The wire mesh sachet can be designed in either a romantic or rustic style.

Aluminum window screening, sometimes called insect screening, is available at hardware stores in shiny silver and dull charcoal gray. For a copper or gold finish, apply an acrylic aerosol paint. Select a potpourri that complements the style of the sachet, adding items such as moss, leaves, pinecones, and wood chips for more variety and texture.

MATERIALS

- Aluminum window screening.
- Potpourri.
- Metallic aerosol paint, optional.
- Utility scissors.
- 2½ yds. (2.3 m) sheer or wired ribbon, for a romantic style.
- Twigs, raffia, and lightweight craft wire, for a rustic style.

HOW TO MAKE A WIRE MESH SACHET

1 Cut two 9" (23 cm) squares of window screening, cutting along weave of mesh. Paint both sides of each piece, if desired, using aerosol paint.

2 Fold back ½" (1.3 cm) along each edge, using a straightedge as a guide.

3 Romantic style. Cut one length of ribbon for each side of screen. Align screen pieces, folded edges together. Using a pencil, poke a hole through both screens at center of each side, ¾" (2 cm) from edge. Through both screens, insert ribbon through holes, and tie in a bow. Fill with potpourri before securing last side.

3 Rustic style. Align the screen pieces, folded edges together. Using craft wire, stitch edges of screens together, adding the potpourri before securing the last side; if necessary, poke small holes with a pencil to aid in inserting wire. Secure twigs along sides of sachet, using wire. Tie a raffia bow at corner.

INDEX

CREDITS

CY DECOSSE INCORPORATED
Chairman: Cy DeCosse
President: James B. Maus
Executive Vice President:
  William B. Jones

CREATIVE ACCESSORIES FOR THE HOME
Created by: The Editors of
  Cy DeCosse Incorporated

Also available from the publisher:
  *Bedroom Decorating, Creative
  Window Treatments, Decorating for
  Christmas, Decorating the Living
  Room, Decorating with Silk & Dried
  Flowers, Decorating the Kitchen,
  Kitchen & Bathroom Ideas, Decorative
  Painting, Decorating Your Home for
  Christmas, Decorating for Dining &
  Entertaining, Decorating with Fabric
  & Wallcovering*

Executive Editor: Zoe A. Graul
Technical Director: Rita C. Opseth
Project Manager: Joseph Cella
Assistant Project Manager: Diane
  Dreon-Krattiger

Senior Art Director: Delores Swanson
Art Director: Linda Schloegel
Writer: Rita C. Opseth
Editor: Janice Cauley
Sample Supervisor: Carol Olson
Photo Coordinator: Diane Dreon-Krattiger
Senior Technical Photo Stylist: Bridget
  Haugh
Styling Director: Bobbette Destiche
Crafts Stylist: Joanne Wawra
Research Assistant: Lori Ritter
Artisans: Sharon Ecklund, Phyllis
  Galbraith, Sara Macdonald, Linda
  Neubauer, Carol Pilot, Nancy Sundeen
*Director of Development Planning
  & Production:* Jim Bindas
Photo Studio Managers: Mike Parker,
  Cathleen Shannon
Assistant Studio Manager: Rena Tassone
Lead Photographer: Mark Macemon
Photographers: Rebecca Hawthorne,
  Mike Hehner, Rex Irmen, John
  Lauenstein, Bill Lindner, Paul Najlis,
  Charles Nields, Mike Parker, Robert
  Powers
Technical Photo Stylist: Susan Pasqual
Production Manager: Amelia Merz
Electronic Publishing Specialist: Joe Fahey

Production Staff: Adam Esco, Melissa
  Grabanski, Mike Hehner, Jeff Hickman,
  Janet Morgan, Robert Powers, Mike
  Schauer, Kay Wethern, Nik Wogstad
Shop Supervisor: Phil Juntti
Scenic Carpenters: John Nadeau, Mike
  Peterson, Greg Wallace
Consultants: Michael Basler, Amy Engman,
  Wendy Fedie, Patrick Kartes, Kathryn
  Kellogg, Tish Murphy, Lindsey Peterson,
  Marlys Riedesel, Suzanne Schumann,
  Donna Whitman
Contributors: American Traditional Stencil;
  Charles Craft; Coats & Clark Inc.; Decart
  Inc.; Dritz Corporation; Dyno
  Merchandise Corporation; Iowa Pigskin
  Expressions; Putnam Company; The
  Singer Company; Stencil Ease;
  Swiss-Metrosene, Inc.; Walnut Hollow
Printed on American paper by: Arcata
  Graphics Company (0495)

Cy DeCosse Incorporated offers a variety of
how-to books. For information write:
  Cy DeCosse Subscriber Books
  5900 Green Oak Drive
  Minnetonka, MN 55343